The *Awakened* Devotional Study Guide For Christian Educators

Also by Angela (Powell) Watson

*The Cornerstone: Classroom Management That Makes Teaching
More Effective, Efficient, and Enjoyable*

Awakened: Change Your Mindset to Transform Your Teaching

The *Awakened*

Devotional Study Guide
For Christian Educators

Angela Watson

Due Season
PRESS
and Educational Services

The Awakened Devotional Study Guide for Christian Educators
by Angela Watson

Published by Due Season Press and Educational Services.

ISBN-13: 978-0-9823127-2-8
ISBN-10: 0-9823127-2-5

Printed in the United States of America.

First Edition

I have not stopped thanking God for you. I pray for you constantly, asking God, the glorious Father of our Lord Jesus Christ, to give you spiritual wisdom and insight so that you might grow in your knowledge of God. I pray that your hearts will be flooded with light so that you can understand the confident hope He has given to those He called—His holy people who are His rich and glorious inheritance (Eph 1:16-18 NLT).

I pray that from His glorious, unlimited resources He will empower you with inner strength through His Spirit. Then Christ will make His home in your hearts as you trust in Him. Your roots will grow down into God's love and keep you strong. And may you have the power to understand, as all God's people should, how wide, how long, how high, and how deep His love is. May you experience the love of Christ, though it is too great to understand fully. Then you will be made complete with all the fullness of life and power that comes from God. (Eph 3:16-19 NLT).

ACKNOWLEDGEMENTS

Is this book really going to resonate with teachers? That's the question I wanted to answer prior to publishing the devotions. I envisioned gathering a little focus group of about 10 people for whom I would post one devotion each weekday on a private blog; their job would be to read it, respond to the questions, and then provide feedback in a comment on the blog post. Nothing earth shattering for me or for them.

As usual, God had other plans. There were *thirty-eight* educators who completed the entire devotional study. The group consisted of brand new teachers (some of whom are still looking for their first job) and veterans who've been in the classroom for as long as 40 years. It included administrators, seminary teachers, substitutes, and paraprofessionals. Almost every grade from PreK-college was represented. Participants included people from all over the United States (including a teacher at a school on an Indian reservation) and even as far away as the Cayman Islands and China. Rural, suburban, and urban schools were represented, public and private, large and small. This is a cross-section of educators that I never imagined gathering together. But each focus group member shares these important commonalities: they love the Lord, and they want to fulfill every purpose He has for their lives, both in their schools and outside of them.

During the focus group study, we all shared a bit of information about our walk with the Lord and our journeys as educators. Each tale was unique and special. This group of educators has been transparent and brutally honest about their faults and shortcomings. We prayed for and encouraged one another continually. It was incredible when participants began posting how they had applied the strategies from *Awakened* and the devotion to their lives, and the positive effects they'd seen. By the end of the 5 weeks, we were all more than a little sad about letting go of the community we'd built. The things God had shown us through each other were precious and life-changing.

It was through the focus group that God called me to lead online Bible studies for this devotional. To my knowledge, it's the first online Bible study developed specifically for classroom teachers and K-12 school-based educators. I look forward to each new group as it begins, and the opportunity to deepen my faith and continue renewing my mind with other educators who are inviting God to do the same work in them.

Here is a list of the participants who completed the focus group study. I truly can't thank them enough for their encouragement and assistance in shaping this book:

Jenny B., 2nd gr. teacher, Salinas, CA
K.B., 4th gr. teacher, Washington, NC
Lisa Berg, 6th gr. teacher, NY
Heather Bergeron, 4th gr. teacher, Crowley, LA
Lee Anne Burton, 2nd gr. teacher, Fairmont, WV
Jessi Caldwell, secondary teacher, Yantai American School, China
Barb Dettmer, kindergarten teacher, Arcadia, MO
Patricia Ewing, paraprofessional, Chillicothe, MO
Tiffany Farrar, 6th gr. teacher, South Dakota Indian Reservation, SD
Sandie Flynn, Ione, CA
Michelle Garrett, 5th gr. teacher, WA

Janet Garrison, para educator, Lexington, KY
Amy Gillespie, elementary teacher, Omaha, NE
Laurie Hagberg, high school teacher, CA
Dana Herndon, elementary teacher, Winder, GA
Lesley Herman, special education teacher, New Castle, PA
Christine Hughes, First Baptist Academy, O'Fallon, IL
Grace Toler, kindergarten teacher
Joni, middle school teacher, CA
Les, administrator, TN
Kesha M., 4th grade teacher, Vidalia, GA
Stephanie Nipper, high school teacher, Sanford, NC
Kathy Noble, kindergarten teacher, Taylor County, WV
Janine Nyyssonen, 5th gr. teacher, Grand Cayman
Leighann Orr, 4th gr. teacher, Worcester, MA
Pamela M. Owen, ECE faculty, Mount Vernon Nazerene University, Mount Vernon, OH
Lynn Wallin Parker, 3rd gr. teacher, Las Vegas, NV
Teresa Pickett, 2nd gr. teacher, Warner Robins, GA
Michelle Reagan, 4th gr. teacher, Greenville, NC
Michelle Reitmeyer, 3rd gr. teacher, Vista, CA
Sarah Sheppard, 1st grade teacher, Winchester, VA
Erin Shoemaker, 4th gr. teacher, NC
Susan, computer educator, Indianapolis, IN
Grace Toler, kindergarten teacher, Greenville, SC
Barb Trombley, 3rd gr. teacher, St. Croix Falls, WI
Christine Waller, 6th gr. teacher, MT
Nicole Wilborn, 1st gr. teacher, Charleston, SC
Jeannie Williams, teacher, OH

In addition to the wonderful members of the focus group, I would also like to thank my parents, extended family members, friends, and *Awakened* readers for their support and kind words of encouragement. I am incredibly blessed to have such an incredible group of people rooting for and praying for me. My husband, Curtis, has also been an amazing source of strength and wisdom. I can always count on him to tell me what I need to hear, and I am continually grateful for his spiritual leadership, companionship, and unfailing love.

Above all, I thank God for laying the idea for this book on my heart. I had no idea what kind of market there would be for a devotional based on *Awakened*, but I wrote each page in faith, trusting that God had something powerful in store. Seeing what He has accomplished in the lives of the focus group participants was the first bit of proof that His plan is (once again) exceedingly, abundantly above all that I could ask, think, or imagine. I can't wait to see what He does next in their lives, in mine, and in the lives of every person who seeks Him through this devotional study. The words of James from over 2,000 years ago continue to ring true: draw near to God, and He will draw near to you (James 4:8 NKJV); if anyone lacks wisdom, let him ask God, who gives generously to all without fault (James 1:5).

PART ONE:
SETTING THE FOUNDATION FOR A HEALTHY MIND

PART TWO:
BREAKING FREE OF DESTRUCTIVE HABITS

PART THREE:
CULTIVATING A POSITIVE FRAME OF REFERENCE

WARNING

This is not a short and sweet devotional book that you can read for thirty seconds each morning right before your students come barreling into the classroom. I like those kinds of devotions. I read them. I even write them sometimes on my blog (devotions.TheCornerstoneForTeachers.com). But that format serves a different purpose; it's for quick bursts of inspiration and short reminders of God's word.

This book is about equipping you for transformational change. It's for tearing down strongholds and breaking through destructive patterns you've been trapped in for years.

When you finish this book, with God's help, you can have a complete renewal of your mind.

And anything of that magnitude takes work.

You've got to be willing to dedicate time and energy to transformational change. It's not always easy to reflect on moments when you were stressed out or experiencing unpleasant emotions. But inviting God into the process means you can think about those things in a productive way. David wrote in Psalm 139:23, "Search me God, and know my heart; test me and know my anxious thoughts." Through prayer and study of God's word, you can learn from your past mistakes and expose the bad mental habits that lead you away from the Lord. Then when those thoughts and habits creep back up, you'll be armed for the battle and ready to take every thought captive.

The more time you give God, the more He can work in you. Our modern society wants a drive-through break-through. God doesn't work like that. Revelation requires time spent seeking Him out, meditating on His word, and being still long enough for Him to speak.

If you're not used to having a few minutes of quiet time alone with God on a regular basis, it will be an adjustment for sure. But I guarantee that it will deepen and change your relationship with Him forever.

And that will change everything else.

Ready to start the journey?

HOW TO USE THIS BOOK

This devotional study guide is designed to correspond with the book *Awakened: Change Your Mindset to Transform Your Teaching*, which is also by me, Angela Watson. There's no right way or wrong way to read these books. The study guide isn't a "read your Bible through in a year" highly structured system (which for me, seems to turn into "read your Bible through in three years, skipping the genealogies and pretty much the entire book of Numbers.") You don't even need to create a schedule for the devotional guide if that's something that will turn into another item on your to-do list and cause you to feel stressed out when you fall behind. Pray about it and figure out a system that works for you.

If you're a person who *does* like a structured approach, here are a few ideas:

- **Read one chapter in *Awakened* and the corresponding devotional each *day*.** You'll have completed both within a month, and with 26 lessons, that even gives you a few days to slack off. You could also read one each *weekday* and be finished in about 5 weeks. If you're ready for transformational change in your life and don't want to spend another moment in bondage to your bad habits, get started right away and push through each chapter on a daily basis with God's help.

- **Read one chapter in *Awakened* and the corresponding devotional each *week*.** This is nice because it gives you time to really absorb what you've read and allow God to work on your heart as you start applying the new ideas to your life. It's also a good approach if you have other Bible studies or Christian books you're currently reading. Here's an idea for a weekly schedule:

   Monday: Respond to the opening reflection and read the chapter in *Awakened*.
   Tuesday: Read the devotion and additional scripture.
   Wednesday: Re-read the devotion and respond to the application questions.
   Thursday: Complete the to-do activity and read the prayer.
   Friday/Weekend: Re-read the prayer and memorize the scriptures from the devotion.

- **Read *Awakened* in its entirety, then tackle the devotional book.** That way you'll have the big picture in your head before starting the devotions, and then have a chance to dig in more deeply and examine how the book lines up with the word of God. Maybe you read *Awakened* several months (or longer) before getting the devotional guide; just skim back over an *Awakened* chapter, asking God to refresh your memory about things He already showed you and open your heart to new insights, then dig in to the corresponding chapter in this book.

- **Use both books with a book club or Bible study.** Many of you have weekly or bi-weekly get-togethers with other teachers at your school to read devotions and share prayer requests. Using this devotional together can be a great way to build a supportive group of believers who pray for and encourage one another through the transformation process.

In conjunction with these options, you can join the online Bible study I facilitate for this devotional: check out my website (TheCornerstoneForTeachers.com/books/awakened-devotional) for more information. The online study provides discussion opportunities with other Christian educators from around the world.

Ultimately, my advice is *just get started*. Don't worry about how you're going to make everything work. Follow God's leading, and take it one day at a time.

Choosing to work through the ideas in this book and apply them to your life requires moment-by-moment decisions. It means looking at the pile of laundry waiting to be folded on the sofa and choosing to take 15 minutes to be alone with God before tackling it. It means resisting the siren's call of the television and finding a quiet space to read God's word instead. Make that decision as often as you possibly can, until it becomes such a routine in your life that you can't imagine going without that time with God. Don't think too much about it. *Just start*. You can do it, with God's help.

Angela

A Note About Scripture References

All scripture is taken from the New International Version (NIV) unless otherwise noted. Information about this translation and others cited is located on the copyright page.

Some translations capitalize pronouns referring to God and others do not. For consistency purposes throughout this book, all pronouns referring to God have been capitalized.

PART ONE:

SETTING THE FOUNDATION
FOR A HEALTHY MIND

INTRODUCTION

HOW I LEARNED EVERYTHING THE HARD WAY:

FOCUSING ON YOUR CALLING

Reading in *Awakened*

Pgs. 1-7

Opening Reflection

What does the Bible have to say about God's view of children? How do you think God views the teaching profession and those who work with young people for a living?

Notes

What God's Word Tells Us

The desire to teach is something that God laid on my heart a long time ago. I remember playing school with my friends and imaginary students, and holding the pages of my books up high so the stuffed animals could see as I asked them questions. Whether your story is similar or you entered the profession later in life, at some point you could probably relate to that feeling of being drawn to our field, or having a sense that you could make a difference in the lives of kids by working in education.

Whatever your role and however you got to the point you're at today, you can be certain that God has a plan to use you in powerful ways through your position as an educator. 1 Peter 4:10-11 says, "Each of you should use whatever gift you have received to serve others, as faithful stewards of God's grace in its various forms. If anyone speaks, they should do so as one who speaks the very words of God. If anyone serves, they should do so with the strength God provides, so that in all things God may be praised through Jesus Christ." God has equipped you with unique gifts and talents so that you can bless and serve others, and *He* provides the strength you need for using them.

Though we may realize the importance of our calling on an intellectual and spiritual level, discouragement tends to creeps in when the everyday tasks drag us down and distract us. There are so many moments when the job of serving others as a teacher does not feel like an honor and special privilege from God. When you're wiping sticky fingerprints off your cabinets or filling out a discipline referral form for a misbehaving student, it's easy to lose sight of why you're in this field. You may not be able to see how certain tasks are important to God. Maybe you figure that God doesn't care about stuff like how you get kids to pay attention during a lesson, so you try to handle the situation in your own strength. Or you might think He doesn't need to be involved in grading papers, so you stop depending on the special equipping God has blessed you with and grumble your way through on your own.

The solution? You can refocus and return to the call on your life through your relationship with God. When you intentionally reconnect with Him, He will reconnect you with the higher purpose He has planned. 1 Corinthians 10:31 says, "Whatever you do, do it all for the glory of God." He wants to be involved in every aspect of your work! The Lord will empower you to meet the needs of each one of your students. He will give the strength to withstand the pressure that comes at you from every direction. He will never leave or forsake you (Heb 13:5).

To stay focused on your calling, don't worry about the mistakes you made yesterday or get hung up on your shortcomings. Just keep pressing toward the goal of knowing Jesus Christ and being transformed into His image. Look forward to seeing whatever God has next for you, and trust Him to equip you to handle every task. The apostle Paul says it this way in Philippians 3:12-14 (NLT): " ... But I press on to possess that perfection for which Christ Jesus first possessed me. No, dear brothers and sisters, I have not achieved it, but I focus on this one thing: Forgetting the past and looking forward to what lies ahead, I press on to reach the end of the race and receive the heavenly prize for which God, through Christ Jesus, is calling us."

Application Questions

What is your teaching testimony? How has God grown you and taught you through your work?

What are the unique abilities God has given to you which help you do your job well? How is God using your gifts and talents in your work as an educator?

patience, compassion, creativity

What has God shown you about your purpose at your school? Are there any particular areas in which you know He wants to use you to bless others or to make school a better place for kids?

Additional Scripture

We have different gifts, according to the grace given to each of us. If your gift is prophesying, then prophesy in accordance with your faith; if it is serving, then serve; if it is teaching, then teach; if it is to encourage, then give encouragement; if it is giving, then give generously; if it is to lead, do it diligently; if it is to show mercy, do it cheerfully.

(Rom 12:6-8)

Add your own here:

"To Do" Challenge

Make a T-chart below. On the left side, list the aspects of being a teacher that you are naturally good at. On the right side, list the tasks and responsibilities that are harder for you to do well or take pleasure in doing. Reflect and pray over this chart, asking the Lord to go before you in the aspects of your work that are more difficult and equip you to do them well. You might also want to compare your chart with a colleague, and see if there is any way you can help bear one another's burdens by helping with tasks that you are each better equipped to do. If you are completing this study on your own, consider approaching a colleague with a "task swap" so that s/he can relieve you of one of the more stressful aspects of your job and you can help him or her with a disliked task, as well.

Glows	Grows
·work with students	· IEP writing
	· testing
	· ULS

Prayer: *Dear Father, I thank You for showing me my calling and for the gifts and talents you have given me. I want to become a more effective educator so that You can use me to my fullest potential. Please help me exercise self-discipline as I pursue this devotional guide, and give me the wisdom to hear what You are trying to tell me. Wipe the slate clean of my sins and clear my mind of distractions so that there is nothing separating me from You, and so I can focus on the work You want to do in me. Help me to keep an open mind and heart. Thank You for all the ways You have grown me and sustained me thus far in my journey. I trust in You and thank You for continuing that good work.*

11/29

CAN YOU REALLY CHANGE THE WAY YOU RESPOND TO STRESS?

CELEBRATING THE PROCESS OF TRANSFORMATION

Reading in *Awakened*

Pgs. 8-18

Opening Reflection

What is the biblical process for self-improvement?

What role does God play in the process of our mental, emotional, and spiritual development?

Notes

What God's Word Tells Us

It's not easy to change our perception of our work or go against our natural reaction to stressful situations. Taking on the challenge of personal transformation can feel pretty daunting. Sometimes Christians refer to the process as sanctification: the process of becoming holy as God as holy. Yikes! That's a pretty intimidating standard. The good news is that we don't have to go through the process in our own strength. We have God's word, the Holy Spirit, and the support of other believers to help us shift our outlook and become more like Christ.

The ultimate goal of transformation is spelled out in Romans 12:2 (NIV 1984): "Do not conform any longer to the pattern of this world, but be transformed by the renewing of your mind. Then you will be able to test and approve what God's will is—His good, pleasing and perfect will." The goal of renewing your mind is to bring your thinking in line with God's. Then you'll be able to understand your purpose and calling as a teacher and as a man or woman of God. You'll be open to different ways He wants to use you, and be able to sense His leading through the Holy Spirit.

It's God desire that all of us would do the work required for transformation: "You were taught, with regard to your former way of life, to put off your old self, which is being corrupted by its deceitful desires; to be made new in the attitude of your minds, and to put on the new self, created to be like God in true righteousness and holiness" (Eph 4:22-24). Anything that God commands us to do *is* possible for us. He never asks us to do anything that we can't accomplish through His power and grace. So if the Lord tells us to put off our old ways of thinking and get a new attitude, we can be assured that this is an attainable goal!

The important thing to remember is that the process of transformation is never-ending. There will never come a day when we wake up and find that we are no longer tempted to be self-indulgent and centered on our own needs. Instead, as 2 Corinthians 3:18 (NKJV) reminds us, we are transformed from "glory to glory." The NIV version says we "are being transformed into His likeness with ever-increasing glory, which comes from the Lord, who is the Spirit."

So each "glory" or level brings us a little closer to God's perfect ideal—and it should be celebrated! The ongoing nature of this process draws us nearer to the Lord on a daily basis and is an opportunity for us to grow in our love for Him and deepen our faith. Even though changing our perception and mental habits can be difficult, God's word assures us that we can be confident in this: He who has begun a good work in you will carry it on to completion until the day of Christ Jesus (Phil 1:6)!

Application Questions

What are some ways you create your own stress?

- Thinking I have no control how I react to events.
- Trying to be "perfect"
- Procrastinate

What supports have you (or could you) put in place to help with the transformation process?

- Tell friend/sponse about my efforts to change my negative thinking so they can help hold me accountable/remind me that I can choose how to react to every situation.

What does a "renewed mind" mean to you? How will you know that your mind is being renewed?

- Rested, open, happy, focused on positive
- Feeling gratitude
- Think before reacting

Additional Scripture

Behold, You desire truth in the inward parts, and in the hidden part, You will make me to know wisdom. Purge me with hyssop, and I shall be clean; wash me, and I shall be whiter than snow. Make me hear joy and gladness, that the bones You have broken may rejoice. Hide Your face from my sins, and blot out all my iniquities.

Create in me a clean heart, O God, and renew a steadfast spirit within me. Do not cast me away from Your presence, and do not take Your Holy Spirit from me. Restore to me the joy of Your salvation, and uphold me by Your generous Spirit.

(Ps 51: 6-12 NKJV)

"To Do" Challenge

Divide the area below into three columns. In the first column, write down two or three of the biggest or most frequent causes of stress for you at work. In the middle column, reflect on how you usually respond to these stressors—maybe you seek comfort in food, or lash out angrily at others, or complain incessantly. In the third column, write your goals: what response to each stressor will you re-train yourself to have, with God's help? These goals can be healthier, more Biblical courses of action that you want to become habitual, such as going to God immediately in prayer, breathing deeply and clearing your mind, exercising, distracting yourself, and so on. You can add to that third column as you continue working your way through the devotional and the Lord shows you more techniques to use.

Causes of Stress	Usual Responce	Re-train goal
• Thinking I need to be perfect, (i.e not meeting a deadline) →	• Frustrated, over-react →	→ Remind myself I'm a work in progress
		Pray, ask for help
		Choose to think in ways that produce joy and contentment

✱ Pray every hour - gratitude
✱ Memorize scripture weekly.
✱ 5 things your thankful for.

Ester 4:14
Perhaps this is the moment I've been created for.

Prayer: *Dear Lord, I thank You for calling me into relationship with You! I am so grateful that I don't have to face the problems and stress of this life on my own. Thank You for loving me right where I am now, and yet inspiring and equipping me to come up higher. Help me to be made new in the attitude of my mind and put off my old self. Allow me to truly see and celebrate each level as you transform me from glory to glory! Help me to love myself the way You love me and be patient with myself in this process. Deepen my faith and fill me with Your grace and power. Thank You, Jesus, for working through me!*

STOP UNWANTED THOUGHTS FROM RUNNING RAMPANT:

PUTTING ON THE FULL ARMOR OF GOD

Reading in *Awakened*
Pgs. 19-28

Opening Reflection
Why are Christians called to "bring every thought into captivity to the obedience of Christ" (2 Cor 10:3-6 NKJV)? What does that phrase mean to you?

Notes

What God's Word Tells Us

The things that are happening right in front of us tend to steal the majority of our attention: a misbehaving child, a ringing phone, or a demand from an administrator. It's sometimes easier to ignore the need for dealing with our unwanted thoughts because those don't exist in the physical realm. But our thoughts are not something that exist *entirely* within our own minds. They are very real and present: combating unwanted thoughts is part of our spiritual warfare.

Ephesians 6:12 (KJV) tells us, "We wrestle not against flesh and blood, but against principalities, against powers, against the rulers of the darkness of this world, against spiritual wickedness in high places." The forces of deception and temptation—from within us and externally—will always continue to try to enslave us. Reminding ourselves of this truth is critical for the journey of transformation. Because we're not facing a problem that is ours alone, we don't have to solve it alone. We have heavenly forces fighting on our behalf!

We are reminded of this in 2 Corinthians 10:3-6 (NKJV): "For though we walk in the flesh, we do not war according to the flesh. For the weapons of our warfare are not carnal but mighty in God for pulling down strongholds, casting down arguments and every high thing that exalts itself against the knowledge of God, bringing every thought into captivity to the obedience of Christ … "

Unproductive thoughts should not run freely and randomly through our minds: we are in a battle, and victory can be won only by taking every thought captive. Our thoughts do not control us, but we can allow Christ to control our thoughts. We have the mighty weapons of God at our disposal to destroy speculations and arguments that are contrary to His truth.

Just as a solider wouldn't show up for battle without his armor and weapons, so we cannot show up for work each day without our *spiritual* armor and weapons. Ephesians 6:14-18 continues by telling us, "Stand firm then, with the belt of truth buckled around your waist, with the breastplate of righteousness in place, and with your feet fitted with the readiness that comes from the gospel of peace. In addition to all this, take up the shield of faith, with which you can extinguish all the flaming arrows of the evil one. Take the helmet of salvation and the sword of the Spirit, which is the word of God. And pray in the Spirit on all occasions with all kinds of prayers and requests. With this in mind, be alert and always keep on praying for all the Lord's people."

Application Questions

What are some instances in which you have allowed critical, bitter, or unkind thoughts to take hold in your mind?

What excuses have you made for these negative thought patterns—how have you justified them to yourself?

What is one step you can take starting right now to stand firm against those thoughts and bring them under the control of Christ?

Additional Scripture

My soul, wait in silence for God only, for my hope is from Him. He only is my rock and my salvation, my stronghold; I shall not be shaken. On God my salvation and my glory rest; the rock of my strength, my refuge is in God. Trust in Him at all times, O people; pour out your heart before Him; God is a refuge for us.

(Ps 62:5-8 NAS)

"To Do" Challenge

You can tap into the powerful imagery of spiritual armor by making the concept more concrete. Start replacing your unwanted thoughts with a visualization of yourself putting on the full armor of God. Envision your unproductive and impure thoughts being blocked by the belt of truth and the breastplate of righteousness. See yourself walking in the shoes of the gospel of peace. Hold an image in your mind's eye of yourself placing the helmet of salvation on your head, and taking up the shield of faith and sword of the spirit. You might even want to sketch this out to create a visual reminder: draw yourself as a simple stick figure and add each of the pieces of armor, labeling them as you read through the verse and repeat it to yourself. Look back to your drawing or mental image when your negative thoughts take hold, and use it to remind yourself that as a child of God, you are *never* defenseless against unwanted thoughts!

Prayer: *Dear Lord, keep me ever mindful that I am in a spiritual battle. Help me to take my negative thoughts seriously and vigilantly defend myself against them. Equip me with the spiritual weapons and armor You've shown me through Your word. Help me to be alert to challenges and distractions that weaken me. Show me how to guard my mind so I can identify and cast down every thought I have that is contrary to your holiness. Remind me that I don't have to do this alone—the battle belongs to You, and I can claim victory in You. Thank You for the other believers You have placed in my life to help me, and for Your word which strengthens me and shows me how to live.*

FOUR STRATEGIES FOR THINKING ON PURPOSE:

SETTING YOUR MIND ON THINGS ABOVE

Reading in *Awakened*

Pgs. 29-36

Opening Reflection

Is it sinful to *think* unbiblical thoughts, or just to *dwell on* them?

Where do you draw the line?

Notes

What God's Word Tells Us

Most of our destructive thoughts come from being too focused on what's happening right now in the physical realm. We get discouraged by the mounds of paperwork in front of us, or worked up over a rude statement made by a parent, student, or colleague. Colossians 3:2 tells us plainly: "Set your minds on things above, not on earthly things." We are to look to the Problem-Solver instead of the problem. And we are called to remind ourselves of how good God is, and recount all the times that He has come through for us. When we make that concerted effort to keep our focus on God and how He is working, we can see things through a healthier, eternal perspective.

Anytime you're dealing with a problem, ask yourself, *How does God see this issue?* and consciously shift your viewpoint so that it aligns with His. If a thought is really bugging you, write down the truths of a Godly perspective. Look up relevant scriptures and include them in your reframing so that you speak the power of God's word over your situation. Re-read the biblical perspective to yourself so that you repeat a holy viewpoint in your mind rather than your own fleshly opinions. Keep your focus on the character of God and your goal of becoming transformed into His image.

Philippians 4:8 provides some additional helpful guidelines for how to think on purpose and with intention: "Finally, brothers and sisters, whatever is true, whatever is noble, whatever is right, whatever is pure, whatever is lovely, whatever is admirable—if anything is excellent or praiseworthy—think about such things." Anytime we set our minds on ideas that meet these criteria, we can experience peace, joy, and contentment. And if we find that we are not experiencing those emotions, we know to examine our thoughts and make sure they line up with the word of God.

For example, if you notice yourself thinking, *My situation at school is impossible–I can't stand this another minute!*, dismiss it by telling yourself, *This thought is not of God. It's not worth thinking about.* Distract yourself by turning your attention to your task in the present moment and asking God to equip you to handle it. Reject any deception that the enemy brings to your mind (*I refuse to obsess over a problem I cannot control*) and replace the lies with God's truth (*God is my vindicator, my refuge, and my strength.*)

Fill your mind with thoughts of the greatness of our God. Claim His promises. Repeat His truths over and over. Hide His word in your heart that you might not sin against Him. Everything about Him and His word is true, noble, right, pure, lovely, admirable, excellent, and praiseworthy. And the more we fill our minds with those things, the more naturally our thoughts will mirror His.

Application Questions

Which of the four strategies for thinking on purpose come easiest to you? Which seem the hardest?

Why do you think that is?

Think of an issue (big or small) that keeps you from experiencing joy and contentment recently. What thoughts about the issue keep you from experiencing God's peace in the midst of your problem?

What is the Godly way of thinking about that issue?

How could the four strategies help you regain an eternal perspective in that situation and keep your mind set on things above?

Additional Scripture

Put to death, therefore, whatever belongs to your earthly nature: sexual immorality, impurity, lust, evil desires and greed, which is idolatry. Because of these, the wrath of God is coming. You used to walk in these ways, in the life you once lived.

But now you must rid yourselves of all such things as these: anger, rage, malice, slander, and filthy language from your lips. Do not lie to each other, since you have taken off your old self with its practices and have put on the new self, which is being renewed in knowledge in the image of its Creator. Here there is no Greek or Jew, circumcised or uncircumcised, barbarian, Scythian, slave or free, but Christ is all, and is in all.

(Col 3:5-11)

"To Do" Challenge

Revisit your negative emotions chart and the stressors chart you created previously. Can you apply the strategies of dismiss, distract, reject, and replace to any of those situations? Make notes about some replacement thoughts you can use when those situations reoccur. You might realize that you've already been using these techniques intuitively, and now you need to name and consciously focus your attention on them: *I am choosing to dismiss that thought. I am rejecting that thought.* Making yourself aware of how you respond to unwanted thoughts and labeling the strategies you're using will strengthen your confidence in handling these situations, and make it easier for you to respond in a healthy way the next time.

Prayer: *Precious Jesus, I come before you today with a humble heart, knowing that far too often, I get caught up in my own thoughts and desires instead of imitating You. I know that my heart and mind are too often divided. Teach me Your way, O Lord, that I may walk in Your truth; unite my heart to fear Your name (Ps 86:11 ESV). Clear away the thoughts and attitudes that aren't of You, and give me a heart after Your heart. Help me to think on purpose, and keep my mind stayed on You. Empower me to fix my eyes not on what is seen, but on what is unseen; remind me that what is seen is temporary, but what is unseen is eternal (2 Cor 4:18). Thank You, God, for the work You are doing in me! Let it all be for Your glory.*

HANDLING THE EMOTIONAL RESPONSE TO STRESS:
RECOGNIZING THAT JOY IS OUR STRENGTH

Reading in *Awakened*

Pgs. 37-42

Opening Reflection

Is it possible to be content or even joyful at all times?

If so, how?

Notes

What God's Word Tells Us

I remember learning a song as a child based on Nehemiah 8:10: "The joy of the Lord is your strength." The words were solidified in my mind, but it took me many years to really understand the power of them. Nehemiah explained that when we're feeling weak—uninspired, discouraged, and lacking enthusiasm—we have a strong tower of strength that is always present. We need to take our eyes off our problems and focus them on God, and our joy will be renewed.

Joy is not optional for Christians. It's not something we just sit around and hope to experience one day when our problems go away, nor is it a luxury that we can't afford to prioritize. Joy is the very foundation of our witness to other people! A depressed or stressed-out Christian is too preoccupied with his or her own needs to have a heart open to opportunities to bless and serve others. If we allow ourselves to become emotionally drained from minor irritations and the endless hassles of daily life, we'll miss out on the selfless acts that God uses to deliver us from our joyless mindset and place us back into the contentment that comes from communion with Him.

So even in our most despondent times, we have to *choose* to tap into the joy that brings us strength. James 1:2-4 (ESV) instructs us to have a spirit of rejoicing in all things: "Count it all joy, my brothers, when you meet trials of various kinds, for you know that the testing of your faith produces steadfastness. And let steadfastness have its full effect, that you may be perfect and complete, lacking in nothing." A student disrespects you? Count it all joy. The photocopier jams so you can't prepare your materials for the day's lesson? Count that as joy, too. The possibility of not having a job next year? That, too! Even the most serious trials we experience can be counted as joy.

It sounds crazy, and sometimes feels impossible. But don't miss the reason James gives us: purposefully stirring up feelings of joy makes us more steadfast in the Lord. By keeping a good attitude, we're actually immunizing ourselves against future stress and making it easier to handle whatever happens next. So if and when a tougher problem occurs, it will actually be *less* difficult for us to deal with because we won't be at the mercy of our emotions. Instead, we'll be stable and immovable. The emotional roller coaster will slowly come to an end as our up-and-down feelings are replaced with the joy that comes from knowing we have everything we need in Christ.

James continues in verses 5-6, telling us *how* to make the choice to behave wisely instead of getting wrapped up in our emotions: "If any of you lacks wisdom, let him ask God, who gives generously to all without reproach, and it will be given him. But let him ask in faith, with no doubting, for the one who doubts is like a wave of the sea that is driven and tossed by the wind." If you are drowning in your emotions and feeling overwhelmed by stress, bring that issue to God. Ask Him for the wisdom to be unwavering and for the maturity to count it all joy, being confident in His promise to guide and uphold you.

Application Questions

What 5 adjectives would you use to describe your natural temperament or your innate personality?

Has your personality or temperament changed as you've grown in your Christian walk? How?

What trials has God used to teach you about maintaining your emotional stability and "counting it all joy"?

Additional Scripture

You, God, are my God, earnestly I seek You; I thirst for You, my whole being longs for You in a dry and parched land where there is no water. I have seen You in the sanctuary and beheld Your power and Your glory. Because Your love is better than life, my lips will glorify You.

I will praise You as long as I live, and in Your name I will lift up my hands. I will be fully satisfied as with the richest of foods; with singing lips my mouth will praise You. On my bed I remember You; I think of You through the watches of the night. Because You are my help, I sing in the shadow of Your wings. I cling to You; Your right hand upholds me.

(Ps 63:1-8)

"To Do" Challenge

Pray about your negative emotions and ask God to give you insight about the thoughts that create them. Then divide the area below in half, labeling the left side "Negative Emotions" and the right side "Negative Thoughts." On the left side, list a few instances from today or yesterday when you felt angry, discouraged, or frustrated. Then see if you can identify the thoughts that created those emotions and jot those down on the right side. For example, maybe you snapped at the people around you during a feeling of extreme irritation, and that feeling stemmed from dwelling on a mental list of all your problems or all the ways you've been mistreated. It may not be easy to remember what you were thinking about, but it's important to recall your general line of thinking so that when those same thoughts pop up again, you'll recognize the emotions they lead to and be on guard. After completing the activity, identify some thoughts that lead to joyful feelings and practice meditating on those ideas instead.

Prayer: *Lord, help me remember that my emotions do not define me. My identity is found in Christ Jesus, and You tell us in Your word that there is no condemnation for those who are in Christ (Rom 8:1). Lord, I don't understand why everything happens in our lives, but You do. Give me faith to trust You when You tell me to count it all joy. Remind me that my trials and tribulations are not cause for stress: they are only momentary, and they are creating an eternal weight in glory (2 Cor 4:17). Thank You for teaching me and testing me. Thank You for loving me enough to call me up to a higher level.*

HOW TO LIVE BEYOND YOUR FEELINGS:

WEAKENING THE FLESH AND STRENGTHENING THE SPIRIT

Reading in *Awakened*

Pgs. 43-52

Opening Reflection

What signals tell you whether you're following your fleshly feelings or the wisdom of the Spirit?

Notes

What God's Word Tells Us

Don't you despise that feeling when you *know* what you should be doing, but just don't *feel like* doing it? You know you're going to look back with regret on how you spent your time and the decisions you made. But it's too hard to go against what you feel in the moment. We all go through life wishing we could make decisions based on what's best for us instead of getting caught up in the way we feel. The struggle is so universal we even find Paul mentioning it in his letter to the church over 2,000 years ago: "I do not understand what I do. For what I want to do I do not do, but what I hate I do" (Rom 7:15).

Human beings have always experienced a conflict between the flesh and the spirit. And we always will, until the day of Christ's return when we are complete and made perfect in Him. This world is not our home, and we will never be free from sin here, because we were created with a fleshly nature and a spiritual nature. "The sinful nature wants to do evil, which is just the opposite of what the Spirit wants. And the Spirit gives us desires that are the opposite of what the sinful nature desires. These two forces are constantly fighting each other, so you are not free to carry out your good intentions" (Gal 5:17 NLT).

That verse explains why we cannot just go through life passively, doing whatever we feel like and letting our emotions determine how we behave. Our feelings come from fleshly desires—to be comfortable, to be recognized and exalted, to have our every whim catered to. The flesh opposes the spirit, which stands firm in truth and wants to do what is right no matter what.

So how can you weaken the power of the flesh? With the same method that's guaranteed to kill *anything*: you stop feeding it. Don't give in to the temptation to dwell on fleshly thoughts or indulge in habits that you recognize as contrary to the work the Spirit is doing in you. If you know that visiting a certain co-worker's room after school will result in a lengthy gossip session that leaves you feeling depressed, start a new routine when school's out and fill your time in a positive way. If wasting time surfing the internet at work causes you to be irritated and unprepared when teaching, shut your computer down when you don't need to be using it.

Remember, you can never choose once and for all to be a completely disciplined person, but you can choose in this very moment not to give your flesh anything that strengthens it. And in the next moment, make that choice again. And again. When you fall short, ask for forgiveness and choose to follow the Spirit in the next moment. God *designed* our walk with Him to be a moment-by-moment battle, because He never wants us to try to do life on our own. What He wants more than anything is for us to look continually to Him in all that we do. And what could be more satisfying than to spend every day of our lives with our hands and faces upturned to our Savior, beholding His glory and marveling not at the intensity of the battle before us but at the magnificence of a war that is already won?

Application Questions

How is your decision making affected by your moods?

At what times are you are particularly vulnerable to following your flesh?

What habits or routines in your life serve to strengthen your flesh?

What new habits can you create that will weaken your flesh?

Additional Scripture

Those who live according to the flesh have their minds set on what the flesh desires; but those who live in accordance with the Spirit have their minds set on what the Spirit desires. The mind governed by the flesh is death, but the mind governed by the Spirit is life and peace. The mind governed by the flesh is hostile to God; it does not submit to God's law, nor can it do so.

Those who are in the realm of the flesh cannot please God. You, however, are not in the realm of the flesh but are in the realm of the Spirit, if indeed the Spirit of God lives in you.

(Rom 8:5-9)

"To Do" Challenge

Consider a time when you felt extremely stressed out. What type of physical stress reaction was created in your body? What were the emotions you felt that contributed to that reaction? Try to record the negative thoughts that caused those emotions to spiral out of control. For example, you might have had panic attack symptoms or sleepless nights because you felt incapable of handling everything that was happening in your life. That feeling of being overwhelmed, powerless, and hopeless might have been the result of thinking critical thoughts about yourself and repeatedly telling yourself that you are incompetent and worthless. Practice living beyond your feelings and following the Spirit by writing out a new way of thinking. Revisit the set of thoughts that triggered your stress reaction and write out the way you could respond to those thoughts if they surface again. Use the model at the bottom of page 50 in *Awakened* to help you if needed.

Prayer: *Lord, help me to develop wise habits based on the leading of Your Spirit rather than my own fleshly feelings. I want to make wise decisions that I will be satisfied with later on. But I know I can't do that on my own. I need You to guide me. Show me how to make moment-by-moment decisions that honor you. Keep me from feeling discouraged when I don't live the way I want to. Remind me that in Your eyes, it's never too late for me to get back on the right path. Thank You for sending the Holy Spirit to dwell in me and be my helper in discerning the right things to do. Father, I ask you to continue purifying my mind and my heart. I want less of me and more of You. Fill me with Your love and Your Spirit. Thank You, Jesus!*

PART TWO:

BREAKING FREE OF
DESTRUCTIVE HABITS

HABIT 1

THINKING NEGATIVELY ABOUT YOURSELF:

FORMING YOUR IDENTITY IN CHRIST

Reading in *Awakened*

Pgs. 53-58

Opening Reflection

What is the proper biblical attitude toward one's self?

Notes

What God's Word Tells Us

When I think about the Bible's teachings on self-image, the term *humility* comes to mind. The first scripture I recall is Romans 12:3: "For by the grace given me I say to every one of you: Do not think of yourself more highly than you ought, but rather think of yourself with sober judgment, in accordance with the measure of faith God has given you."

The first part of that verse is frequently quoted, but there's a hidden gem in the second half. When we think of ourselves with "sober judgment," it shouldn't be our *own* judgment based on our *own* criteria ... it should be "in accordance with the measure of faith" that God has given us. And that faith tells us some very powerful things about the way the Lord sees each one of us. Are you ready for this?

You have been chosen by God and adopted as His child (Eph 1:3-8). You are God's workmanship (Eph 2:10). You've been established, anointed, and sealed (2 Cor 1:21-22). You have been appointed to bear fruit (John 15:16). You are a branch of Jesus Christ, the true vine, and a channel of His life (John 15:5). You've been bought with a price, and now you belong to God (1 Cor 6:19-20). You've been redeemed and forgiven of all your sins (Col 1:13-14). You were washed clean and justified in the name of Jesus (1 Cor 6:11). And now, you are complete in Christ (Col 2:9-10) and you have direct access to the throne of grace through Him (Heb 4:14-16).

That is the source of our identity as believers. We are the blood-bought sons and daughters of the king! So being humble does *not* mean having a low self-opinion. When you criticize yourself, you're tearing down the precious child of God whom Jesus gave up His life for. All the things that secular society values most—such as our appearance, wealth, and status—are actually the least important part of our identities. Even when we succeed in those areas, they pale in comparison to what Christ did on the cross and what He's continuing to do today, through us and through others. That's where our focus should be! Galatians 6:14 (NKJV) puts it this way: "But God forbid that I should boast except in the cross of our Lord Jesus Christ, by whom the world has been crucified to me, and I to the world."

Instead of thinking and speaking negatively about yourself, repeat the biblical components of your identity and the characteristics you acquired because of Christ. *He* is the core of our identity and self-perception, not the way we think, talk, and act, and not the things we have accomplished ourselves. We have to separate our *who* from our *do*! We can be humble about the things that we've done, and be proud of what Christ has done in us. Everything good inside of us comes from God, so we can boast freely in Him!

Application Questions

What negative beliefs about yourself have you attached importance to and validated as truth?

How have your behavioral habits and actions reinforced those negative beliefs in your mind?

What are some examples of "extreme language" you frequently use that exaggerate your problems?

What are some healthier, more accurate ways you can restructure those thoughts?

What can you do to better align your self-image with the way God sees you?

Additional Scripture

Not that we dare to classify or compare ourselves with some of those who are commending themselves. But when they measure themselves by one another and compare themselves with one another, they are without understanding …

Let the one who boasts, boast in the Lord. For it is not the one who commends himself who is approved, but the one whom the Lord commends.

(2 Cor 10:12, 17-18 ESV)

"To Do" Challenge

Choose one or two of the negative beliefs you identified in the first application question on the previous page. Think about what solution-oriented questions you can ask yourself instead of repeating those self-deprecatory ideas (pg 56 in *Awakened*). For example, if you constantly berate yourself for being absent-minded, replace those criticisms with questions like, *How can I keep track of the things I need to do?* and *How can I make it easier to remember my tasks?* When you're tempted to be overly hard on yourself, focus on asking the right questions and putting your solutions into place so that you can improve in those areas slowly over time.

Prayer: *Dear Lord, help me not to compare myself to others or to some vision I've created in my own mind of how I'm "supposed" to be. I've read over and over in Your word that I am precious beyond compare: help me to believe that. Let it sink deep down into my soul so that I see myself the way You see me. Give me the wisdom to reject the lies my mind tells me, and return to Your truth. Help me to have a right and balanced self-image so that my identify is rooted in You. Keep me humble, Jesus. Keep my eyes ever focused on You. I love You, Lord! Thank You for loving me first, and showing me how to love myself.*

Habit 2

EXPLAINING SETBACKS IN A PESSIMISTIC WAY:

TRAINING YOURSELF TO SEE THINGS GOD'S WAY

Reading in *Awakened*

Pgs. 59-68

Opening Reflection

Can a pessimistic outlook ever be honoring to God?

Why or why not?

Notes

What God's Word Tells Us

Maybe you're realizing that you've adopted an increasingly pessimistic outlook over the course of your career. Who hasn't heard themselves mutter things like, "I just *knew* that whole plan would fall apart/the funding wouldn't come through/they'd create some ridiculous new mandate. These things never work out! Teaching just gets harder every year. It's impossible to do this job now—and wait until next year!" In many ways, it's true that the demands on teachers and the needs of students have intensified over the years, and therefore it's very easy to fall into the trap of becoming jaded.

Pessimism can function as a defense mechanism. To many people in the world, it's a perfectly acceptable and completely realistic outlook. Pessimism is so common that we may not even question it except in the most extreme situations. However, normal doesn't always equal healthy, and it certainly doesn't equal Godly. We know that there is no part of God's being that worries, dreads, or fears. He is love, and love hopes all things and believes all things. The God we serve can turn a negative situation around at any time! He is always in control, and He has overcome the world (John 16:33), so we have no reason to be pessimistic about the future. When we choose to ignore this fact and dwell on a negative perspective, we are actually working *against* God and forfeiting the power that comes from dwelling in Him.

Learning to replace our negative explanations with Godly truth requires less time spent soaking up worldly influences and more time spent in the word. We need to meditate on the Bible and memorize it to benefit fully. David wrote in Psalm 119:11, "I have hidden Your word in my heart that I might not sin against You." Scripture is the most powerful weapon we have to discern and counter a negative, pessimistic attitude: "For the word of God is living and active, sharper than any two-edged sword, piercing to the division of soul and of spirit, of joints and of marrow, and discerning the thoughts and intentions of the heart" (Heb 4:12 ESV).

As much as we'd like it to, a cursory glance at the Bible during a weekly church service just isn't enough to allow scripture to permeate our way of thinking and shift our outlook on life. James 1:23-25 tells us to *look intently* into the word and then continually act on it: "Anyone who listens to the word but does not do what it says is like someone who looks at his face in a mirror and, after looking at himself, goes away and immediately forgets what he looks like. But whoever looks intently into the perfect law that gives freedom, and continues in it—not forgetting what they have heard, but doing it—they will be blessed in what they do."

I challenge you to wake up each morning and set your focus on obeying God's word by praying Psalm 19:4 (ESV): "Let the words of my mouth and the meditation of my heart be acceptable in Your sight, O Lord, my rock and my redeemer." As you go through the day, speak scripture over each pessimistic thought you have. When you feel like a situation is hopeless, proclaim that all things are possible with God (Matt 19:26). When you worry that things will never get better, claim the promise that God works ALL things together for the good of those who love Him and are called according to His purpose (Rom 8:28). When you fear being helpless to improve your situation, speak the truth that our God is a mighty warrior who saves (Zeph 3:17). You can replace every negative explanation of setbacks with biblical truths in full confidence because of God's proclamation in Isaiah 55:11 (NLT) that His word will never return void: "I send it out, and it always produces fruit. It will accomplish all I want it to, and it will prosper everywhere I send it."

Application Questions

Which aspects of a pessimistic explanatory style do you tend to exhibit?

How does that pessimistic outlook affect you? Your spiritual walk? Your effectiveness as an educator?

What replacement thoughts can you use to counter your pessimistic explanatory style with the truth of God's word?

Additional Scripture

This Book of the Law shall not depart from your mouth, but you shall meditate on it day and night, so that you may be careful to do according to all that is written in it. For then you will make your way prosperous, and then you will have good success. Have I not commanded you? Be strong and courageous. Do not be frightened, and do not be dismayed, for the Lord your God is with you wherever you go.

(Josh 1:8-9 ESV)

"To Do" Challenge

Scripture memorization doesn't have to be an arduous, time-consuming process: just meditate on (think about and repeat) a verse, and it will naturally become a part of your self-talk. Remember, that's the same process that got those *negative* thoughts to take hold in your mind! You are capable of memorizing anything you think about a lot. Start by actively searching for two or three scriptures that you can repeat instead of a negative outlook. You can select verses from this devotional, or use an online concordance to help you search by topic or keyword. Copy the scriptures that are most meaningful to you and re-read them each morning as you start your day. After several days, try saying them with your eyes closed, opening to peek at the words as needed. You'll soon notice that the scriptures will become "hidden in your heart" so that you can not only say them each morning without looking, but also recall large portions of them throughout the day when you are tempted to be pessimistic.

Prayer: *Dear Jesus, I ask You humbly to give me a heart like David's in Psalm 119. I want to delight in Your word! Drown out those worldly influences that weaken my desire for the things of the spirit. Help me to form new habits so that I look forward to spending time with You, and so that there is none on earth that I desire more than You (Ps 73:25). Lord, let Your word be a lamp for my feet, and a light for my path (Ps 119:105). I am so grateful that You have given Your inspired word to teach me what is true and to make me realize what is wrong in my life (2 Tim 3:16 NLT). Correct me, teach me, mold me. Show me the futility of my pessimistic explanations and replace them with a hope and a peace that comes only from knowing You. I love you, Father!*

Habit 3

Replaying and Rehearsing Conflicts:

Breaking Free of Condemnation

Reading in *Awakened*

Pgs. 69-73

Opening Reflection

John 8:36 says, "So if the Son sets you free, you will be free indeed."

What does it mean to be free in Christ?

Notes

What God's Word Tells Us

One of the most exhausting and frustrating things my mind does is focus immediately on criticism and problems. I can spend hours organizing my classroom, but when I picture it in my head, my focus goes straight to the corner I didn't have time to clean. I can have 20 productive and positive conferences and then lay awake at night thinking about the *one* person who hinted at something that could *possibly* be construed as somewhat negative. I can think back on my teaching career and perfectly envision all the times and places I lost my temper with a student, was embarrassed in a meeting, or had a disagreement with a colleague. And for many years, each time those thoughts came into my head, *I let them stay there.*

I'm still grappling with the fact that replaying and rehearsing conflicts is a bitter trap that God wants to see all His children break free from. I constantly remind myself that my thoughts are just thoughts, and my feelings are just feelings, but the *truth* is that Jesus' sacrifice on the cross rescued us from both self-condemnation and the trap of condemning others. Romans 8:1-2 tells us, "There is now no condemnation for those who are in Christ Jesus, because through Christ Jesus the law of the Spirit who gives life has set you free from the law of sin and death." Dwelling on conflicts of any kind is a dead mindset, but the Spirit gives us life! We have been set free from thinking about all the mistakes we and others have made.

I love what Galatians 5:1 (NKJV) tells us: "Stand fast therefore in the liberty by which Christ has made us free, and do not be entangled again with a yoke of bondage." Choosing to rehearse conflicts and replay problems is equivalent to a slave being set free and then deciding, "Nah, I'd rather keep those chains on. Let me refasten them." Each time we dwell on a past problem that we've already taken before God, we are choosing to tighten those chains just a little bit more. And yet, Jesus stands before us, His hand outstretched as He holds the key. It's our choice whether to reach out and receive His offer to unlock our chains.

Jesus died on the cross not only for our *eternal* salvation, but to keep us from being slaves to sin in *this* lifetime. We have the freedom to let go of the things in our past that we've already asked Him to forgive. We don't have to replay conflicts and problems because in His eyes, all sincerely confessed sins have been forgotten. Psalm 103:12 (NLT) reminds us that no matter how far we go in pursuit of dredging up past mistakes, we will never reach them: "He has removed our sins as far from us as the east is from the west."

When you are tempted to replay and rehearse conflicts, replace your thoughts with scriptures that remind you where past mistakes and heartaches lie in God's sight. Isaiah 1:18 says we have been washed clean: "'Come now, let us reason together', says the Lord. 'Though your sins are like scarlet, they shall be as white as snow; though they are red as crimson, they shall be like wool.'" Micah 7:19 has another powerful visual about where our past lies: "You [God] will again have compassion on us; You will tread our sins underfoot and hurl all our iniquities into the depths of the sea." Bring your thoughts into agreement with God: we are free from our past and our mistakes are forgiven, to be remembered no more.

Application Questions

What problems, disagreements, or arguments do you frequently replay in your mind?

What is your goal when replaying or rehearsing conflicts—what does your mind tell you can be accomplished by doing that?

What is the biblical way to accomplish that goal?

What practical steps can you implement to help you take the biblical approach instead of your fleshly reaction?

Additional Scripture

For those who live according to the flesh set their minds on the things of the flesh, but those who live according to the Spirit set their minds on the things of the Spirit. For to set the mind on the flesh is death, but to set the mind on the Spirit is life and peace.

For the mind that is set on the flesh is hostile to God, for it does not submit to God's law; indeed, it cannot. Those who are in the flesh cannot please God. You, however, are not in the flesh but in the Spirit, if in fact the Spirit of God dwells in you …

For you did not receive the spirit of slavery to fall back into fear, but you have received the Spirit of adoption as sons, by whom we cry, "Abba! Father!" The Spirit himself bears witness with our spirit that we are children of God, and if children, then heirs—heirs of God and fellow heirs with Christ, provided we suffer with Him in order that we may also be glorified with Him.

(Rom 8:5-9, 15-17 ESV)

"To Do" Challenge

Choose one of the conflicts you jotted down for the first application question on the previous page and pray about how you can reframe it. Ask God to show you the positives in the situation and give you a healthy perspective. Write down your reframing (you can use pgs. 71-73 in *Awakened* to give you ideas.) Try to incorporate scripture so that you're replacing your negative thoughts with the power of the living word. Read your reframing whenever you find yourself getting drawn into thinking about conflicts. You may want to underline one or two key sentences or phrases to memorize, and say them aloud to yourself whenever you're alone: while driving in the car, walking, making dinner, cleaning the house, etc. This will retrain your mind to recall your reframing whenever you think about the conflict and prevent you from mindlessly rehashing the situation.

Prayer: *Dear God, I ask You first and foremost to forgive me of my sins. Show me any unconfessed sin I have in my life and convict me. Lord, I also ask that You help me release those mistakes to You so that I don't feel compelled to hold on to them anymore. Wash me as white as snow. Remove my sins, my shame, my self-condemnation as far as the east is from the west. I'm claiming Your promise that I am now dead to my past and free of the bondage of replaying my shortcomings over and over in my head. Thank You, Jesus, that by Your wounds I am healed (Isa 53:4-5)! I am set free, Lord, even when I don't feel like I am. Remind me that my feelings have no power over Your word. I choose in this moment to stand fast in the liberty by which Christ made me free. Help me to make that choice again and again, Lord.*

Habit 4

Holding on to Past Resentment:

Receiving Healing From God

Reading in *Awakened*

Pgs. 74-79

Opening Reflection

In what ways has God already healed and restored you?

What circumstances or events did He use?

Notes

What God's Word Tells Us

Chances are, today's reading in *Awakened* had you thinking about deep-seated issues that have nothing to do with teaching—probably issues that first occurred before you even became an educator. And yet your perception of your past affects your current identity on every level. The way you think about and treat yourself now as a result of your past can impact the way you treat your students, the way you relate to your colleagues and superiors, and your entire perception of your role in the classroom. Healing those old wounds and having a healthy perspective on them can make a huge difference in your ability to teach well and forge relationships with others in your school.

I don't have to convince you that letting go of the past would be beneficial. But you're probably wondering where to go from here, and the process of dealing with painful memories is not exactly something you're looking forward to. Fortunately, for the follower of Christ, the solution to our problems is never really about us and the things *we* need to do. It's about God and what He has already done … and what He still wants to do in and through us. The process of healing from our past is centered less on doing and more on receiving. Grace and redemption are rightfully ours already as the inheritance of God's children, if we choose to receive them (Eph 1:3-14).

The most important step in the biblical process of healing and restoration is to go continually before the Lord in humility. James 4:7-10 (NKJV) instructs us, "Therefore submit to God. Resist the devil and he will flee from you. Draw near to God and He will draw near to you. Cleanse your hands, you sinners; and purify your hearts, you double-minded … Humble yourselves in the sight of the Lord, and He will lift you up." Recognize before God that dwelling on feelings of helplessness, bitterness, and self-pity is contrary to His word. Ask forgiveness for those times and tell God you want to want to feel His healing power and claim His promise of restoration (I love the line, "Lord, I believe! Help my unbelief!" from Mark 9:24 NKJV.) Acknowledge your dependence on Him and invite Him to work in you.

Ask these things in faith, speaking God's healing over your life even when you don't feel it happening. God's words "bring life to all who find them and health to all their flesh" (Prov 4:20-22 NKJV). Your feelings will eventually follow your thoughts, and God will change your heart over time. Maintain a feeling of hope and optimism, trusting that God has promised to give us double blessings in *this* lifetime for our former trouble: "Instead of your shame, you will receive a double portion, and instead of disgrace, you will rejoice in your inheritance. And so you will inherit a double portion in your land, and everlasting joy will be yours" (Isa 61:7).

Remind yourself that healing and restoration is usually a process, not an overnight miracle, and be content in this, knowing that all things happen in God's perfect timing. As you pray the prayer of faith, "do not become sluggish, but imitate those who through faith and patience inherit the promises" (Heb 6:12 NKJV). Continue to recognize that we can't change the past or direct the future: the present is the only time we have any control over. And it is up to us to choose, right now in this moment, to focus on how God is sustaining, healing, restoring, and blessing us.

Application Questions

How has your perception of your past become a part of who you are? How does it affect your thoughts and emotions in the present?

How does your relationship with your past affect your teaching?

What is your experience with "digging in the bottomless pit" of your past? To what extent is it helpful for you to work through bad memories?

Are there any factors (medical diagnoses, family traits, etc.) that make you feel helpless and unable to break free from your past?

Additional Scripture

Trust in the Lord and do good; dwell in the land and enjoy safe pasture. Take delight in the Lord, and He will give you the desires of your heart. Commit your way to the Lord; trust in Him and He will do this: He will make your righteous reward shine like the dawn, your vindication like the noonday sun.

Be still before the Lord and wait patiently for Him; do not fret when people succeed in their ways, when they carry out their wicked schemes. Refrain from anger and turn from wrath; do not fret—it leads only to evil.

(Ps 37:3-8)

"To Do" Challenge

You may be realizing that elements of your past have a stronghold in your life: an area of extreme darkness that creates ongoing spiritual, emotional, or mental problems (2 Cor 10:4-5). If so, consider seeking out additional resources, or make an appointment to talk with a leader at your church. There are many Biblical tools for receiving healing from strongholds: you can pray in agreement with others (Matt 18:18-20), have church elders pray over you and anoint you with oil (James 5:14), and pray alone while fasting as an act of humility (Ezra 8:21). Notice that each one of these approaches is centered around prayer. So, compose a clear vision of what healing means to you so that you can see how God is answering your prayer. *How would your daily life be different if you were to be healed from the residual effects of your past?* Meditate on that. Write down what that means to you, and humbly make your request known before God.

Prayer: *Father, I don't want to let the bad things in my past keep me from having a good future. I don't want anything to stand in the way of You accomplishing Your plan for my life. Help me to stop thinking about (and acting out on) the things that happened in the past, and focus instead on the work You're doing right now in me. Lord, I'm sorry for the times I let my self-pity and hopelessness overshadow the truth that I am perfect and complete in You. Restore me, Lord. Make me whole. Loose the bonds of my strongholds. Destroy every false argument that has set itself up against Your word. Through the blood of Jesus I have been set free of my past. I claim healing and restoration over every aspect of my life. I speak these things in faith knowing that they will be answered in the name of Jesus Christ. Thank You, Lord! All the glory, honor, and power is Yours.*

HABIT 5

TAKING THINGS PERSONALLY:

CHOOSING TO BE TENDERHEARTED

Reading in *Awakened*

Pgs. 80-85

Opening Reflection

How is God using the things that offend you to make you more like Him?

Notes

What God's Word Tells Us

Our God is a holy God, and we know He calls us to be holy, as well. But many of us have never thought about the stark contrast between His holiness and our tendency to take things personally or become easily offended. Here's the connection: every time we sin and fall short of God's standard of holiness, we grieve the Holy Spirit. That means we are grieving—or offending—God innumerable times each and every day. Read what Ephesians 4:29-31 says about this: "Do not let any unwholesome talk come out of your mouths, but only what is helpful for building others up according to their needs, that it may benefit those who listen. And do not grieve the Holy Spirit of God, with whom you were sealed for the day of redemption. Get rid of all bitterness, rage and anger, brawling and slander, along with every form of malice."

Whenever we choose to be self-centered or resentful or speak unkindly about others, we are offending the God we love and serve. And yet He never gives up on us. He understands that we rarely do things with the intention of hurting or disrespecting Him, and He doesn't hold a grudge while waiting for us to finally realize what we've done. Our heavenly Father continues to look on us with love and favor and grace even when we are oblivious to our shortcomings and behaving foolishly. In light of this, how can we possibly be annoyed with others when they inadvertently offend us?

The next verse in Ephesians tells us how to behave instead: "And be ye kind one to another, tenderhearted, forgiving one another, even as God for Christ's sake hath forgiven you" (Eph 4:32 KJV). I love the word *tenderhearted*. It's so easy to be hardhearted, isn't it? It makes sense to our fleshly reasoning when we choose to act coldly toward an inconsiderate administrator or an insolent student. We feel justified in drawing ourselves up haughtily because we don't believe we deserve to be treated as we have been.

And yet God calls us to cultivate tender hearts that respond to others' needs with grace and edifying words. Since that's not a natural reaction in our flesh, we can't simply wait until we *feel* tenderhearted toward someone. Most of the time, it's not going to happen spontaneously! We have to *choose* to behave in a tenderhearted way. I don't think we can begin to comprehend how important this is to God. Our relationships with one another are a big deal: it is truly the desire of our Father's heart to see His children bearing with one another in love (Col 3:13-15). He delights in seeing us handling conflicts with mercy and understanding, just like we take pleasure in seeing our students behave that way.

Instead of taking things personally when people treat you poorly, stir up compassion, empathy, and grace within yourself. Ask God to help you think tenderhearted thoughts and be as patient with others as He is with you. Place your focus on understanding and meeting other people's needs. As Philippians 2:1-5 (ESV) implores us, "So if there is any encouragement in Christ, any comfort from love, any participation in the Spirit, any affection and sympathy, complete my joy by being of the same mind, having the same love, being in full accord and of one mind. Do nothing from rivalry or conceit, but in humility count others more significant than yourselves. Let each of you look not only to his own interests, but also to the interests of others. Have this mind among yourselves, which is yours in Christ Jesus."

Application Questions

What habits in your life are signs that you've lost sight of God's holiness and the volume/magnitude of your offenses toward the Holy Spirit?

Have you ever tried waiting for a low mood to pass before responding to an offense, or allowed the situation to resolve itself instead of immediately reacting? How does that work for you? How can you remind yourself to try this strategy more often?

What habits can you build—or what truths can you meditate on—to set your intent each morning for treating people with patience and kindness (instead of waiting to see how they treat you and responding accordingly)?

Additional Scripture

To You, O Lord, I lift up my soul. O my God, I trust in You; let me not be ashamed; let not my enemies triumph over me. Indeed, let no one who waits on You be ashamed; let those be ashamed who deal treacherously without cause.

Show me Your ways, O Lord, teach me Your paths. Lead me in Your truth and teach me, for You are the God of my salvation; on You I wait all the day. Remember, O Lord, Your tender mercies and Your loving kindnesses, for they are from of old. Do not remember the sins of my youth, nor my transgressions; according to Your mercy remember me, for Your goodness' sake, O Lord.

Good and upright is the Lord, therefore He teaches sinners in the way. The humble He guides in justice, and the humble He teaches His way. All the paths of the Lord are mercy and truth, to such as keep His covenant and His testimonies.

(Ps 25:1-10 NKJV)

"To Do" Challenge

The Bible tells us to bless those who persecute and hurt us (Rom 12:14)—not only for their sake, but for ours, so that we can have peace and restore our relationship with a holy God. Fight against your flesh now and say a prayer for the person at school who offends you more often than anyone else. Ask God to give you a tender heart toward him or her. Then create a plan for how to take the radical step of making that person's life better. What can you do tomorrow to show that person support and meet his or her needs? Choose one thing you can do, and implement it. The next time you're offended, pray again and choose another act of grace. Each time you are dealt unkindness, turn the other cheek and repay the offense with more kindness. It's not easy to do, but you can try this strategy for just one week. Then reflect on the effect it's had on your peace of mind, stress level, and relationship with God … and perhaps even your relationship with the person who frequently offends you.

Prayer: *God, I ask You to show me people's underlying needs that cause them to act out. Help me to actively look for ways to fill those needs, rather than focusing on what the person is doing or not doing for me. Thank You for showing so much patience toward me even when I do the same foolish things over and over again. I'm so grateful that I have that model of how to behave. Help me to walk in the light as You are in the light (1 John 1:7), and shine into the darkness that is around me. I accept the challenge of behaving in a tenderhearted, compassionate way even when I don't feel like it, and I trust You to change my attitude over time as You mold me into Your image, from glory to glory. Thank You, Father.*

HABIT 6

MISPLACING RESPONSIBILITY:

WORKING AS UNTO THE LORD

Reading in *Awakened*

Pgs. 86-94

Opening Reflection

What are the benefits of working to serve the Lord instead of working to serve people?

Notes

What God's Word Tells Us

Sometimes we take on more responsibility than we should. At other times, we neglect our responsibilities, procrastinating and passing them off on others. In both situations, Ephesians 6:7-8 can give us a quick attitude check: "Serve wholeheartedly, as if you were serving the Lord, not people, because you know that the Lord will reward each one for whatever good they do." Our work as teachers is not just something we do to get a paycheck. It's not even just something we do to contribute to society or help children. *We teach for the Lord.*

That principle was not established to be a burden or foster a legalistic attitude: *Geez, I can't leave work five minutes early even though no one's paying attention—God is watching and He's my real boss. I wish I only answered to an earthly authority.* Nor does it mean that the Lord requires you to work 16 hours a day and come home exhausted and full of guilt for not meeting every need of all the people in your life.

Rather, working unto the Lord means that the earthly and the divine are intertwined. Having that mentality lends a sense of sacredness to every menial task we complete. Instead of, *How little can I get away with doing?* our perspective becomes, *How much do I get to do in order to feel more connected with God and honor Him?* Instead of, *I have to do everything myself to keep this place running smoothly!* your outlook becomes, *What does God want me to get done today, and how can I keep Him first in my mind and heart while I work?*

When we grade papers, we can choose to work with an attitude of reverence toward God, knowing He has given us the task and is pleased when we tackle it without complaint. When we patiently explain something to a child for the seventy-seventh time, we have the satisfaction of knowing we have shown honor toward God by not considering ourselves too busy to help with something trivial. No matter how monotonous we might consider a task, it glorifies God when we do it with sincerity of heart. Colossians 3:23-24 says that when we work to serve Christ, we will be richly rewarded! "Whatever you do, work at it with all your heart, as working for the Lord, not for human masters, since you know that you will receive an inheritance from the Lord as a reward. It is the Lord Christ you are serving."

Working unto the Lord is the solution to our habit of misplacing responsibility. It means choosing to move away from an attitude of blame shifting or self-condemnation and faithfully completing whatever job God has given you in the moment. When you work unto the Lord, God will speak softly into your heart, reminding you that He has entrusted you with the work and will empower you to do it. Invite the Lord into your daily tasks and ask Him to make them more enjoyable and meaningful. Allow Him to open your eyes to see your job the way He sees it: as an opportunity to be the physical representation of Christ in your classroom.

Application Questions

In what ways do you tend to get out of balance with personal responsibility? Can you identify the areas in which you take on too much and the areas in which you take on too little?

Who are the people in your life that collude with you—those who share and reinforce your unhealthy thinking patterns? What role do you play in those collusions?

Who are the people that can help you choose to be powerful instead of pitiful? What practical steps can you take to support each other in working unto the Lord?

Additional Scripture

Now we ask you, brothers and sisters, to acknowledge those who work hard among you, who care for you in the Lord and who admonish you. Hold them in the highest regard in love because of their work. Live in peace with each other.

And we urge you, brothers and sisters, warn those who are idle and disruptive, encourage the disheartened, help the weak, be patient with everyone. Make sure that nobody pays back wrong for wrong, but always strive to do what is good for each other and for everyone else. Rejoice always, pray continually, give thanks in all circumstances; for this is God's will for you in Christ Jesus.

(1 Thess 5:12-18)

"To Do" Challenge

Divide the area below into two columns. On the left side, list a handful of self-defeating, self-pitying truisms about teaching that you frequently hear repeated by yourself or others. Some examples include: *Students today have no ability to concentrate. The parents at this school don't care about their kids' education. This school district puts the needs of students dead last.* On the right side, jot down some rebuttals to those statements that accept a healthy, appropriate level of personal responsibility: *I can teach my students techniques for concentrating, and I don't have to become discouraged by the kids who reject my help in this area. I can reach out to parents who want to be involved with the school, rather than assume that none of them care. I can stop dwelling on the test-prep culture created by the school system and focus my energy on making at least some of the assignments I give more relevant and meaningful.* Add to your list of empowering statements as you retrain your mind to avoid self-pity, collusion, and misplaced responsibility.

Prayer: *Lord, I thank You for the opportunity to be salt and light in my school. I choose to see my job as the chance to represent Christ. Please chip away at my laziness and help me to overcome the moments of burn out when I stop caring about my work, and give me a proper perspective on priorities so that I don't swing too far the other way and make teaching my entire life. Surround me with people who lift me up, and empower me to edify them, as well. I invite You into my classroom each day, Jesus. Give me balance. Show me the divine within the mundane. Let me experience each task You give me as something meaningful and beneficial. Father, I choose to serve You whole-heartedly today: fill me with Your Spirit and equip me to work in a manner that brings honor to You.*

Habit 7

Anticipating Problems:

Resting in Jesus

Reading in *Awakened*

Pgs. 95-101

Opening Reflection

What is the "peace that passes understanding" (Phil 4:6-7)?

Notes

What God's Word Tells Us

It's a cherished old hymn: *What a friend we have in Jesus, all our sins and griefs to bear! What a privilege to carry everything to God in prayer! O what peace we often forfeit, o what needless pain we bear, all because we do not carry everything to God in prayer.* There is such wisdom in those words! Think about it: we forfeit our own peace. We bear pain needlessly. And why? Because we choose to create burdens and carry them ourselves rather than entrusting them to God. We think that we need to reason our way through problems, and plan and predict everything that will happen instead of bringing our concerns before the Lord in faith.

Jesus tells us in Matthew 11:28-30 (ESV), "Come to Me, all who labor and are heavy laden, and I will give you rest. Take My yoke upon you, and learn from Me, for I am gentle and lowly in heart, and you will find rest for your souls. For My yoke is easy, and My burden is light." Jesus sacrificed His life for us so that we could have peace. He tells us in this verse that we don't have to carry our own burdens or anticipate everything that will happen, because we can trust in Him. He also calls us to learn from His example of being meek and humble: it's impossible to have peace or rest when you assume you must have all the answers and need to figure everything out yourself. But when you yoke yourself to Jesus, you're connected to Him so that you can work together and share the load.

Philippians 4:6-7 gives us clear instructions for entering the rest Jesus offers: "Do not be anxious about anything, but in everything by prayer and supplication with thanksgiving let your requests be made known to God. And the peace of God, which surpasses all understanding, will guard your hearts and your minds in Christ Jesus."

Supplication simply means telling God what your needs are. Most of us have no problem with that! But don't miss the rest of the sentence. We are called to pray not in a spirit of complaint or desperation or doubt, but in thankfulness, knowing that God sees our needs. He hears our prayers. And He created a solution before we even realized we had a problem. Therefore, we can bring everything to God in prayer; believing, trusting, and resting in Him through faith. By having a grateful heart when we pray in faith, we shift our mindset from that of anxiousness to one of peace.

There is a fourth verse to "What a Friend We Have in Jesus" that I never remembered singing and only recently discovered. I hope these words bring you as much peace as they have brought to me: *Blessed Savior, Thou hast promised Thou wilt all our burdens bear. May we ever, Lord, be bringing all to Thee in earnest prayer. Soon in glory bright unclouded there will be no need for prayer. Rapture, praise, and endless worship will be our sweet portion there.*

Application Questions

In which situations or areas of your life are you particularly prone to anticipating problems?

Was there ever a time when you expected to feel anxious yet were surprisingly calm? What made the difference for you?

What habits in your life need to change in order for you to enter the rest that Jesus speaks of? Use the verses from the devotion and the additional scripture as a mirror to help you examine yourself.

Additional Scripture

Humble yourselves, therefore, under the mighty hand of God so that at the proper time He may exalt you, casting all your anxieties on Him, because He cares for you. Be sober-minded; be watchful.

Your adversary the devil prowls around like a roaring lion, seeking someone to devour. Resist him, firm in your faith, knowing that the same kinds of suffering are being experienced by your brotherhood throughout the world.

And after you have suffered a little while, the God of all grace, who has called you to His eternal glory in Christ, will Himself restore, confirm, strengthen, and establish you. To Him be the dominion forever and ever. Amen.

(1 Pet 5:6-11 ESV)

"To Do" Challenge

List a few specific things that you are worrying about and carrying as a burden right now. Then circle the ones that are anticipated problems—things that you aren't actually facing right now in this very moment and won't have to deal with until later. Choose and write down replacement thoughts that you can pray instead. So next to an anticipated problem thought like, *That student with severe behavior problems might get transferred to my class,* you can write a prayer thought such as, *I cast my cares on You, God, and I thank You for helping me handle whatever students are assigned to my class, today and every day.* You could replace a thought like, *I can't possibly get everything on my list accomplished tomorrow and I'm going to be so exhausted,* with a prayer like, *Lord, I choose to enter Your rest in this moment because I can trust You to give me the grace I need tomorrow.* At the end of this study, you'll have the opportunity to revisit the full list of worries, see which ones came to pass, and reflect on your strategies for coping with them.

Prayer: *Father, You tell me in Your word that You will supply every need of mine according to Your riches in glory in Christ Jesus (Phil 4:19 ESV). I come before You humbly, asking You to teach me to look to You to figure out my future and equip me to handle it. Restore, confirm, strengthen, and establish me, Jesus. I choose to yoke myself to You. I cast all my cares on You, because You care for me. Thank You, Lord, that I don't have to bear all my burdens myself! With Your help, I'm going to replace my anxious thoughts with prayers that You will guard my heart and mind with the peace that passes understanding. Thank You for loving me, for being a friend who sticks closer than a brother, and for the privilege of carrying everything to You in prayer.*

MAKING PRESUMPTUOUS JUDGMENTS:

EXERCISING GODLY DISCERNMENT

Reading in *Awakened*

Pgs. 102-109

Opening Reflection

Is there ever a time when it's okay for Christians to make judgments about other people?
If so, when? If not, why not?

Notes

What God's Word Tells Us

Luke 6:37 (KJV) is one of the most frequently twisted and misinterpreted verses in scripture. Even people who have never picked up a Bible know the first part of this verse and toss it around whenever they feel criticized: "Judge not, and ye shall not be judged: condemn not, and ye shall not be condemned: forgive, and ye shall be forgiven." I've heard colleagues quote this when they feel like someone is telling them how to teach. I've even heard students use it during disagreements with one another: *Don't judge me. You don't know me.* Everyone hates the feeling of being judged by other people. So can making judgments ever be the right thing to do?

Let's look more closely at the words Jesus chose. In this verse, He is telling us not to make a judgment (decision) about a person and condemn them (express disapproval or pronounce them as guilty) because of that judgment. Scripture tells us that God alone knows the heart (1 Kings 8:39), and He is the true judge (Isa 33:22). Since we lack God's omniscience, it's not even worth our time to try to figure out someone's motives or intentions. We can't possibly understand everything that's happened to them and what they were thinking and feeling. Nor do we have the authority to condemn them for it.

What we *can* do is be discerning (use good judgment with insight and understanding). In John 7:24 (NKJV), Jesus instructs us, "Do not judge according to appearance, but judge with righteous judgment." He's telling us not to act on a fleshly presumption of what we *think* is going on based on what we see, but a correct evaluation based upon the word of God. For example, we can exercise righteous judgment by not accepting or sharing in unbiblical teachings (2 John 1:7-11). But we cannot make a judgment about any person's heart, motives, intentions, or character. Romans 14:12-13 is quite clear on this: "So then, each of us will give an account of ourselves to God. Therefore let us stop passing judgment on one another. Instead, make up your mind not to put any stumbling block or obstacle in the way of a brother or sister." As we tell our students: worry about yourself! One day you will have to give an account to God for how *you* acted.

So, we're never supposed to judge what's happening on the inside of people. And there are only two specific times when we are specifically instructed to judge others' *actions*: when determining whether a Christian should become a church leader (1 Tim 3 and Titus 1:7-9), and when a fellow Christian is living in sin (Matt 18:15-17). In that second scenario, we are to confront our brother or sister directly (not talk about them to other people) and do so with a gentle heart full of love, eager to help them get back on God's path (Gal 6:1). Our own heart attitude is a critical element, because it's quite easy to make a correct judgment about someone but to do it with a wrong motive, such as to shame others or exalt ourselves.

That's the extent of our biblical instruction to make judgments about the people around us. I can't help but compare that to the number of times God calls us to have compassion and show grace. The wisest approach is *always* to resist the urge to jump to conclusions, and instead carefully weigh and measure all the evidence before determining how to respond biblically. I urge you to tread carefully in this area, remembering that the measure you use to judge will be the measure used for you (Matt 7:2). When in doubt, err on the side of compassion and kindness. The energy you spend judging someone else for their choices could be used to edify others and help right their wrongs. Keep 1 Corinthians 16:14 (ESV) as your guiding principle: "Let all that you do be done in love."

Application Questions

What behaviors or situations cause you to act judgmental or jump to conclusions about others?

How does this presumptuous, judgmental attitude affect your spiritual life?

How can you tell if a thought is based on Godly discernment or on a fleshly judgment?

Additional Scripture

Therefore you have no excuse, O man, every one of you who judges. For in passing judgment on another you condemn yourself, because you, the judge, practice the very same things. We know that the judgment of God rightly falls on those who practice such things. Do you suppose, O man—you who judge those who practice such things and yet do them yourself—that you will escape the judgment of God?

(Rom 2:1-4 ESV)

"To Do" Challenge

Try recording some of the thoughts that come to mind when you're in the situations you listed for the first application question. Then replace each one with a thought that focuses on examining yourself instead, or thinking something positive about the person you judged. Replace: *She is so heartless and rude to her students!* with *I need to make sure that my words and tone are always kind with my students.* Replace: *This kid is total jerk who thinks he's too cool to participate in class!* with *I have ways of masking my insecurities and weaknesses, too.* When the presumptuous thoughts pop into your head, don't beat yourself up about it. Just choose the very next thought that comes after it, and make sure it's something that reminds you to examine yourself more closely than you examine others. With time, you'll find that your judgmental thoughts are almost immediately followed by kinder, more productive ones.

Prayer: *Dear Jesus, it's my prayer today that no corrupting talk would come out of my mouth, but only what is good for building up, so that I can give grace to everyone who hears me (Eph 4:29 ESV). I don't want to be a judgmental person or a hypocrite: I need You to help me take the plank out of my own eye before I examine the speck in someone else's (Matt 7:5). Keep me humble, Lord, so that I don't presume to know what's going on in other people's hearts and lives or jump to conclusions about the type of people they "really" are. Keep me focused on helping others and building them up instead of tearing them down. Let all that I do be done in love, Father, just like Your thoughts and actions are consistently loving toward me.*

Habit 9

Ruminating Needlessly:

Embracing the Adventure Of Following Christ

Reading in *Awakened*
Pgs. 110-120

Opening Reflection
What is the biblical response to worry?

Notes

What God's Word Tells Us

When we ruminate endlessly on problems in our lives, what we're really trying to figure out is how to make ourselves comfortable. We're trying to anticipate all the bad things that can happen and stop them so we aren't inconvenienced or pained. Often, even when we attempt to "let go and let God," we're still telling Him our opinion of what's best: "Dear Lord, please let this parent conference go smoothly and let Johnny behave and let my principal leave me alone." Sometimes we pray as though our whole goal is just to make the least amount of work for ourselves and cruise through life without any trials.

But consider the example set by the apostle Paul. He writes in 2 Corinthians 11:24-28 (NKJV) that he had been repeatedly beaten and stoned, and was hungry, thirsty, cold, unclothed, and sleepless ... and yet, "what comes upon me daily: my deep concern for all the churches." Other people's spiritual growth would have been the last thing on *my* mind in that situation! But Paul wasn't thinking about his own pain and worrying about what he'd have to suffer through next. He was focused completely on the excitement of being used by God and seeing what He had planned next.

In all of recorded scripture, Paul never once prayed for material things for himself or to be made comfortable. Instead, he asked the churches to join him in praying that he'd have the strength to endure through God's plan. Biblical scholars suggest that Paul wrote many of the epistles while in a prison cell sitting in raw sewage. Yet he didn't pray to be released from his chains, or even that prison conditions would improve. His prayers centered mostly around the needs of others. Read where Paul's mind was fixed in Ephesians 3:16-19: "I pray that out of His glorious riches He may strengthen you with power through His Spirit in your inner being, so that Christ may dwell in your hearts through faith. And I pray that you, being rooted and established in love, may have power, together with all the Lord's holy people, to grasp how wide and long and high and deep is the love of Christ, and to know this love that surpasses knowledge —that you may be filled to the measure of all the fullness of God."

It's not wrong to ask God to improve our circumstances. The Lord cares for us as His children and wants us to enjoy the life Jesus died to give us! But, as Beth Moore once said, "If we remain compelled by comfort, we will miss the greatest adventures of our calling." Following God is not supposed to be an exercise in familiarity. If we want to stop "giving it to God" and then taking our problems back again, we have to truly accept our role in the adventure. We have to believe that God always has something amazing in store, and that difficult circumstances are the chance to know Him on a level that we can't reach when we are stuck in our comfort zone.

God calls us to be content and stay joyful through an abiding faith that He is in control and working on our behalf. The only way to make that a practical reality is to deepen your faith through trials. Sometimes life has to spin so far out of control that you finally come to the end of yourself and learn what it really means to be okay with any outcome, simply because you have no other choice. It's a humbling, desperate, and uncomfortable position to be in, but when our pride is weakened, God can move mightily. We learn for ourselves that anytime a situation seems hopeless and unbearable, we can push through and come out on the other side as a stronger person with deeper faith, truly knowing the love of Christ and filled with the fullness of God, just as Paul prayed over 2,000 years ago.

Application Questions

What are some things you worry about because you are afraid of being uncomfortable?

Are there any "legitimate" worries that you need to plan for, take actionable steps, and then release to God? Record the part that you need to do before stepping back to allow God to do His part.

What are some specific thoughts you can meditate on when you are tempted to ruminate (such as mantras, affirmations, scriptures, or prayers)?

Additional Scripture

We give thanks to the God and Father of our Lord Jesus Christ. He is our Father who shows us loving-kindness and our God who gives us comfort. He gives us comfort in all our troubles. Then we can comfort other people who have the same troubles. We give the same kind of comfort God gives us. As we have suffered much for Christ and have shared in His pain, we also share His great comfort.

(2 Cor 1:3-5 NLT)

"To Do" Challenge

Part of the adventure of following Christ is being open to all the ways He wants to use us. Make a list of what you can do to meet other people's needs: include as many things as you can think of, both big (volunteer in a ministry) and small (call a friend and tell her you're praying for her.) When you get lost in your own problems and your mind feels cluttered, choose something from the list and see how God shifts your perspective so you can see the big picture again. Remember that this will be the opposite instinct of your flesh, which will insist you cannot possibly meet other people's needs when you have your own problems to solve! But "you can be sure that God will take care of everything you need, His generosity exceeding even yours in the glory that pours from Jesus" (Phil 4:19 MSG).

Prayer: *Lord, I know that here on earth I WILL have many trials and sorrows, but I can have peace anyway, because You have overcome the world (John 16:33). I am free to focus on meeting the needs of other people because You will meet MY needs. Help me to stop ruminating and start meditating; stop worrying and start praying; stop thinking about my own issues and start thinking about those of others. Renew me in these areas day by day, Lord. Help me to clear my cluttered mind of unneeded thoughts so that I have mental space for problem solving and for hearing Your still, small voice prompting and guiding me. I accept and embrace Your plan for my life; I trust that You will bless and prosper me, and I choose to accept any discomfort along the way. I want to experience the adventure of trusting and following You. I'm committed to and excited about this journey, Father, wherever You may lead!*

HABIT 10

CLINGING TO PRECONCEIVED EXPECTATIONS:

TRUSTING THE SOVEREIGNTY OF GOD

Reading in *Awakened*
Pgs. 121-126

Opening Reflection
How should we pray for situations we're concerned about?

Is it okay to ask God for a specific outcome?

Notes

What God's Word Tells Us

If you're anything like me, you've got a lot of ideas swirling around your mind about how the world ought to be: Everyone *should* behave this way; things are *supposed to* happen like that. And maybe you're also like me in that you didn't even realize those preconceived expectations were there, and never thought that challenging them had anything to do with your Christian walk. It takes a deep study of the character of God and His plan for creation to see that there's a powerful reason for us to be open to any outcome in any situation. In fact, the body of Christ is empowered like no other to release our attachment to preconceived expectations.

Why? Because we believe in the sovereignty of God (all things are under His rule.) We believe in the providence of God (He cares and provides for all our needs so that we can accomplish His purposes.) Our Lord is omniscient, omnipotent, and omnipresent. He was, and is, and is to come (Rev 1:8). He knows everything that has already happened in the universe and everything that will come to pass. He has called us to Himself in advance and ordained our steps. And so we honor God (and maintain our peace) by surrendering our will to His.

God originally created a perfect world, and it's His desire that everyone would love and serve Him. However, He also gave us free will, or the *option* to serve and obey Him. Forced love is not real love; God didn't design us to be robots, He wanted us to choose Him, and have the ability not to if we wanted. When people don't choose Him and follow their own plans instead, the consequences of sin are felt in the world, and often affect many other people even generations later. These things grieve God as much as they grieve us, but He permits them. Though this might seem like a contradiction that we often struggle to understand, it is the very fact that *He gives permission for us to have tribulations* that forms the foundation of our peace.

Nothing that happens to us is out of God's sovereign will. Every event in your life is Father-filtered. It's *all* designed to work together for the good of those who love Him and are called according to His purpose (Rom 8:28). That doesn't mean every element is good, in and of itself. But when the events of our lives come together in the grand scheme of things, God promises—it will be *good*. You wouldn't want to eat a stick of butter or a teaspoon of salt or a cup of flour by themselves, but you need each of those ingredients to make a cake. They *work together* to create something good.

God's plan is to prosper and not harm us, to give us a hope and a future (Jer 29:11). So we don't have to concern ourselves over which precise outcome comes to pass. We can trust God to give us what He deems best, and the strength to endure any hardship that He allows. Instead of thinking about what you want to happen, concentrate on God and your spiritual development: What is God trying to teach you through your circumstances? How can you bless other people as a result of what you're experiencing? How can you give the glory to Him, whatever the outcome may be? The way to let go of your expectations is always to trust in the almighty God, because He is trustworthy in all situations.

Application Questions

What was the most challenging problem you faced in your past? How has God proven Himself faithful in working the individual "bad" elements together for your good?

What is the biggest challenge in your life right now? How is God using that situation to grow you and make you more like Him?

Are you holding tightly to any preconceived expectations about how your situation "must" be resolved in order for you to be happy? How would your life be different if you chose to trust God and be open to any outcome He provides?

Additional Scripture

O Lord, You have searched me and known me. You know when I sit down and when I rise up; You understand my thought from afar. You scrutinize my path and my lying down, and are intimately acquainted with all my ways. Even before there is a word on my tongue, behold, O Lord, You know it all. You have enclosed me behind and before, and laid Your hand upon me. Such knowledge is too wonderful for me; it is too high, I cannot attain to it. Where can I go from Your Spirit? Or where can I flee from Your presence? …

Your eyes have seen my unformed substance; and in Your book were all written the days that were ordained for me, when as yet there was not one of them …

How precious also are Your thoughts to me, O God! How vast is the sum of them! Search me, O God, and know my heart; try me and know my anxious thoughts; and see if there be any hurtful way in me, and lead me in the everlasting way.

(Ps 139: 1-7, 16-17, 23-24 NASB)

"To Do" Challenge

If you tend to look back on your day and think mostly about unmet expectations and the things that *didn't* go the way you wanted, try making a mental (or written) rundown of all your accomplishments and the good things that happened. Do this whenever you are most inclined to think about things you didn't get done but were "supposed to" (such as when you're leaving work for the day and sigh at the piles of ungraded papers still on your desk) or when you get discouraged from thinking about all that you "must" do tomorrow (such as right before bed when the house is still a mess.) You may find that at least 2 or 3 times a day, it's helpful to pause and reflect on all the things you've gotten done. Then when someone asks how you're doing, all your accomplishments and positive interactions are right in the forefront of your mind so you can share them, uplift others, and give God the glory.

Prayer: *Lord, I always have such great plans in my heart, but You are the One who directs my steps (Prov 16:9). You go before me, and You go behind me. You created me, and You numbered my days. You have counted the hairs on my head (Luke 12:7), and kept all my tears in a bottle (Ps 56:8). No one has ever loved me the way You have, and no one ever could. Keep me as the apple of Your eye; hide me in the shadow of Your wings (Ps 17:8); uphold me in the refuge of Your strong tower (Ps 61:3). I don't need anything but You in order to be happy. Let the world fade away, Lord, so that I see You and You only. More than anything in the world, Jesus, I want Your presence in my life. Fill me with Your Holy Spirit; refresh me, and make me new.*

PART THREE:

CULTIVATING A POSITIVE
FRAME OF REFERENCE

EXAMINE YOUR UNREALISTIC STANDARDS:
ABIDING IN CHRIST

Reading in *Awakened*
Pgs. 127-138

Opening Reflection
Why did Jesus say "Be perfect, therefore, as your heavenly Father is perfect" (Matt 5:48)
if He knew that we can never reach that standard?

Notes

What God's Word Tells Us

Our *shoulds, oughts,* and *musts* are ways that we attempt to exert control over the world. They reflect a prideful heart in which we assume we know best and therefore everyone should meet our standards. But following the Bible's instructions to replace a prideful attitude with a humble dependence on the Lord can break the cycle of creating irrational standards and being disappointed when they're not met. Humbling ourselves before God frees us from our tendency to look to ourselves, others, and our circumstances for happiness, and returns us to the One who is the source of true joy and the giver of life in abundance.

Instead of fighting desperately to make the world conform to our expectations, we can look to God for everything we need. In John 15:1-2, Jesus teaches us, "I am the true vine, and My Father is the gardener. He cuts off every branch in Me that bears no fruit, while every branch that does bear fruit He prunes so that it will be even more fruitful." I love this analogy of God as the gardener who sustains life and makes all growth possible. He will prune the branches in our lives that aren't bearing fruit as well as the ones that *are* bearing fruit so they can produce even more. That means no area of our lives will go untouched! God is constantly growing us. Joyce Meyer likes to say, "You're pruned if you do, and you're pruned if you don't!"

Jesus continues in verses 5-6: "I am the vine; you are the branches. If you remain in Me and I in you, you will bear much fruit; apart from Me you can do nothing. If you do not remain in Me, you are like a branch that is thrown away and withers; such branches are picked up, thrown into the fire and burned." When we get worn out from trying to make the world conform to our standards, we're like a branch that's been removed from the vine. We wither away until there is nothing left, because we've disconnected ourselves from the life-giving source. Jesus tells us to instead *remain* in Him. Another translation is to *abide* in Him, which means *to act in accordance with and accept.* When you're exhausted, spend some time just hanging on the vine. Abide in Christ, cling to Him, soak up His provision, and bask in the tender care of our Father, the gardener, who nourishes and sustains you.

Look at what Jesus then promises us in verses 7-8: "If you remain in Me and My words remain in you, ask whatever you wish, and it will be done for you. This is to My Father's glory, that you bear much fruit, showing yourselves to be My disciples." Here's what Jesus is saying: If we choose to remain in Christ (not in our own understanding), whatever we ask will be done, because the things a Christ-minded person asks for will glorify God and result in fruit bearing.

A branch's purpose is to bear fruit, and that's our purpose, too. It's how we bring glory to God. So anytime we abide in Christ—we think and act in accordance with Him—and ask to bear fruit in His name, God will do it for us. The power of prayer is intended not for our selfish desires, but for fruit bearing. So bring your shortcomings to the Lord: your frustrations, your unrealistic expectations, your cycle of comparison and tendency to evaluate rather than appreciate what He's done. Ask God to prune away those branches and help you bear more fruit so that you can bring glory to Him.

Application Questions

What standards that you hold (for yourself or others) frustrate you most when they're not met?

What are the "branches" that is God is trying to "prune" right now in you?

What fruit bearing is He growing you for?

Are your self-imposed standards hindering the work God wants to do in and through you? How?

In light of your answers above, what area(s) of your prayer life need to change? Are there circumstances that you pray will conform to your standards, instead of asking God to help you bear fruit in whatever conditions He sees fit to orchestrate?

Additional Scripture

Christ is the visible image of the invisible God. He existed before anything was created and is supreme over all creation, for through Him God created everything in the heavenly realms and on earth. He made the things we can see and the things we can't see—such as thrones, kingdoms, rulers, and authorities in the unseen world.

Everything was created through Him and for Him. He existed before anything else, and He holds all creation together.

(Col 1:15-17 NLT)

"To Do" Challenge

You may experience a bad mood when your pessimistic explanatory style makes things seem worse than they are. Then when you compare your inaccurate perception of reality to the unrealistic standards you hold, things seem even worse! But when you perceive yourself and your circumstances the way God sees them, let go of your standards, and open yourself up to God's plan, you will experience peace. Reframe some of your standards from the first application question on the previous page, using examples from the chapter in *Awakened* to help you. Challenge your automatic thoughts by accurately assessing your situation and identifying more rational standards that line up with the word of God.

Prayer: *Lord, I want to let go of my selfish and prideful tendency to make the world conform to my standards, and I want to surrender my will to Yours. I am choosing not to base my happiness on whether I (and the people around me) live up to my self-imposed standards. I can't meet my own standards, much less Your standard of perfection! Let my shortcomings remind me of how much I need You, and draw me closer to You each day. You accept me even though I am not perfect; help me to follow your example and accept myself and others. Remind me that the purpose of my life is not to be comfortable and get what I want, but to bear fruit for You. Jesus, You are supreme over creation; You hold everything together. Not me. It's in You that I live and move and breathe and have my being (Acts 17:28). Thank You for providing for all my needs. I can let go and cast all my cares on You, because You care for me (1 Pet 5:7).*

APPRECIATE THE PRINCIPLE OF SEPARATE REALITIES:

BECOMING A SERVANT TO ALL

Reading in *Awakened*
Pgs. 139-145

Opening Reflection
What do you think Jesus would say about accepting and responding to the differing viewpoints of other people?

Notes

What God's Word Tells Us

The apostle Paul provides a fantastic example of how the principle of separate realities can be applied to the life of a believer. 1 Cor 9:22 tells us Paul *became all things to all people* so that he might save some. The Message translation clarifies this well: "Even though I am free of the demands and expectations of everyone, I have voluntarily become a servant to any and all in order to reach a wide range of people: religious, nonreligious, meticulous moralists, loose-living immoralists, the defeated, the demoralized—whoever. I didn't take on their way of life. I kept my bearings in Christ—but I entered their world and tried to experience things from their point of view. I've become just about every sort of servant there is in my attempts to lead those I meet into a God-saved life … " (1 Cor 9:20-23, MSG).

Paul is clear that he didn't change who he was or compromise the gospel. But he actively worked to understand others' point of view so that he could be in better relationships with them and draw them to God. He maintained this approach with everyone he encountered—not just those who lived less religious and non-religious lifestyles, but also with those who chose to live *more* religious lifestyles than him. Paul didn't try to make other Christians think and act exactly as he did. He didn't present his way of doing life as the model for anyone else. Instead, he was a *servant* to all.

Humility should be our guiding principle when examining separate realities. That means we need to get ourselves off our minds and not allow pride to influence the way we respond to others. Just because we find people with outlooks similar to ours and we collude with them does not mean we're right, or that the Lord is pleased with our attitude: "The Lord detests all the proud of heart. Be sure of this: they will not go unpunished" (Prov 16:5). We are to let God show us what to say to others. Isaiah 50:4 says, "The sovereign Lord has given me a well-instructed tongue, to know the word that sustains the weary. He wakens me morning by morning, wakens my ear to listen like one being instructed." Most of us need to do less talking and more listening to God and other people!

When confronted with someone who has a completely different perspective from you, check your heart attitude before responding. Remind yourself, *I think I'm right, but I could be wrong.* Examine your motives in wanting to correct someone or share your viewpoint. If there is any part of your flesh that is fighting to prove itself right, embarrass or shame the other person for being wrong, or exalt yourself over others, then wait before speaking. Let God soften your heart first so you can respond as His servant instead of as yourself.

It's tempting for us to think we know more than other people, and incredibly easy to inadvertently abuse our position of authority in the classroom. But even though we are smarter than our students in many ways, we don't know everything about their lives or have perfect insight into every struggle they're facing. And though we may have degrees in education, we don't have the right to feel superior to our students' parents and the choices they make in raising their kids. Knowledge puffs up, but love builds up (1 Cor 8:1). The ultimate goals of every interaction should be to edify others, show people the love of God, and ensure He is getting the glory from our relationships and lives. Ask the Lord to help you approach others with this perspective in mind and a deep sense of compassion in your heart. As Proverbs 15:23 (NKJV) reminds us, "A man has joy by the answer of his mouth, and a word spoken in due season, how good it is!"

Application Questions

How do you determine when it's appropriate to compromise/allow others to have their way and when you need to stand your ground?

Can you think of a conflict created in your life because you believe you're viewing things biblically and the other person is not? What would be the healthy way for you to *think* about that situation? How should you *respond* to that person?

During times of minor personality conflicts, what you can think or do to remind yourself that everyone's perception is biased and non-objective so that you approach things in a Christ-like way?

Think of someone in your life whose thought system is more useful and healthier than yours in some aspect. When you don't see eye-to-eye with that person, how can you help yourself adopt their outlook?

Additional Scripture

Welcome with open arms fellow believers who don't see things the way you do. And don't jump all over them every time they do or say something you don't agree with—even when it seems that they are strong on opinions but weak in the faith department. Remember, they have their own history to deal with. Treat them gently ...

Your task is to single-mindedly serve Christ. Do that and you'll kill two birds with one stone: pleasing the God above you and proving your worth to the people around you.

(Rom 14:1, 18 MSG)

"To Do" Challenge

You can experience less frustration and conflict with students when you apply the principle of separate realities. Write down the names of a few students (or other people in your school) who frequently see things differently than you do. Ask God to show you how to understand those people's perspectives and speak a word in due season to them. If a student gets on your nerves with his constant complaining, you may realize he has experienced so much failure that he automatically resists every assignment. How can you edify him in light of this separate reality? If a student often criticizes and tears others down, she may have someone in her life who belittles her. How can you inspire her to speak positive words and develop love for herself and others? Even when you are administering consequences for students' poor behavioral choices, you can still maintain healthy thinking by mentally accepting their separate realities so you are disciplining from love rather than anger and vengeance.

Prayer: *Jesus, I come before You today and ask that You help me to approach others with a servant's heart. You tell us in Your word that pride comes before disgrace, but with humility comes wisdom (Prov 11:2). Give me the wisdom to understand where other people are coming from, and grant me insight as to why they think and act in ways that are at odds with mine. Help me to respond in love, with words that build up rather than tear down. Set a guard over my mouth, Lord, and keep watch over the door of my lips (Ps 141:3). Thank You for loving and accepting me unconditionally so that I can show that same love and acceptance toward others.*

SEPARATE PRACTICAL AND EMOTIONAL PROBLEMS:

GUARDING YOUR HEART AND STAYING ROOTED IN GOD

Reading in *Awakened*

Pgs. 146-152

Opening Reflection

Why is obedience to God so crucial in obtaining freedom from our emotions?

Notes

What God's Word Tells Us

Many of the emotional problems we create for ourselves come from following our feelings instead of following Jesus. We get depressed and overwhelmed when we stop meditating on the truths that all things work together for our good and God will provide for all our needs. We get angry and irritable when we're shaken out of our comfort zones or someone deigns to inconvenience us; we forget that our purpose on this planet is show God's love to others and glorify Him in *everything* we do, no matter how trivial (1 Cor 10:31).

We can choose not to let circumstances and events penetrate our hearts and cause us to feel and behave in ways that are contrary to the word of God. Proverbs 4:23 instructs us, "Above all else, guard your heart, for everything you do flows from it." Your heart is a sacred place that influences every aspect of your life: don't let it be infiltrated by the enemy! "He that has no rule over his own spirit is like a city that is broken down, and without walls" (Prov 25:28 NKJV). But "he that is slow to anger is better than the mighty; and he that rules his spirit, than he that takes a city" (Prov 16:32 NKJV).

The emotional life of a Christian is designed to be a stable one. Psalm 1:1-3 (ESV) tells us to be like a tree that is firmly planted, ready to bear fruit: "Blessed is the man who walks not in the counsel of the wicked, nor stands in the way of sinners, nor sits in the seat of scoffers, but his delight is in the law of the Lord, and on His law he meditates day and night. He is like a tree planted by streams of water that yields its fruit in its season, and its leaf does not wither. In all that he does, he prospers." Notice that prosperousness is a result of guarding one's heart against ungodly influences. Emotional stability comes from spending time meditating on God's word, not from talking to ungodly people about our problems and complaining.

Jeremiah 17:5-10 uses a similar analogy: "Cursed is the one who trusts in man, who draws strength from mere flesh and whose heart turns away from the Lord … But blessed is the one who trusts in the Lord, whose confidence is in Him. They will be like a tree planted by the water that sends out its roots by the stream. It does not fear when heat comes; its leaves are always green. It has no worries in a year of drought and never fails to bear fruit. The heart is deceitful above all things and beyond cure. Who can understand it? I the Lord search the heart and examine the mind … " God is sending us a clear message here: it's not our emotions that we can trust, it's Him. And when our confidence is in the Lord, we will never fail to bear fruit, regardless of the circumstances we face.

When we are mindful of the emotions we feel and refuse to allow them to create additional problems, we can truly experience the liberty and freedom that come from abiding in Jesus. Philippians 1:28-29 says, "Whatever happens, conduct yourselves in a manner worthy of the gospel of Christ … stand firm in the one Spirit, striving together as one for the faith of the gospel without being frightened in any way by those who oppose you." You have the mind of Christ (1 Cor 2:16), and you can remain emotionally stable through *anything* God allows in your life.

Application Questions

In what circumstances is it hardest for you to maintain emotional stability?

In what ways do you need to be more vigilant about guarding your heart against ungodly influences?

When you have an emotional response to a practical problem, what can you do to get yourself "planted like a tree" emotionally before responding to the practical problem?

Additional Scripture

For the Lord gives wisdom; from His mouth come knowledge and understanding. He holds success in store for the upright. He is a shield to those whose walk is blameless, for He guards the course of the just and protects the way of His faithful ones.

Then you will understand what is right and just and fair—every good path. For wisdom will enter your heart, and knowledge will be pleasant to your soul. Discretion will protect you, and understanding will guard you.

(Prov 2:6-11)

"To Do" Challenge

Create a small three column chart like the ones in the *Awakened* chapter: one column for the practical problem, one for the first emotional problem, and one for the second emotional problem. Choose a reoccurring event in your life that creates stress or bad moods for you, and identify your thoughts during that situation. For example, if the practical problem is that students are constantly late to class, write down the first emotion(s) that the circumstance creates in you (*I feel disrespected and angry that I have to spend my time catching students up*), and then how you respond to those emotions (*I can't let the feeling go and everything those students do just makes me angrier.*) Underneath the chart, write how you could talk yourself through that issue the next time it happens: outline a positive response to the second emotional problem and work backward until you have solved the practical problem. Use the examples on 149-152 in *Awakened* and the scriptures from the devotion to help you.

Prayer: *Lord, I acknowledge before You today that my life is not about getting my way and avoiding inconvenience; it's about glorifying You. Convict and prompt me to avoid things that strengthen my flesh so that I can rule over it instead of allowing it to rule over me. Give me a hunger and thirst for Your word so that I can be rooted firmly in You. Guard my heart, Father. Help me to be well balanced, temperate, and sober of mind, withstanding the enemy and being firm in faith against his onset—rooted, established, strong, immovable, and determined (1 Pet 5:8-9 AMP). Lord, You tell us in Psalm 91:1 (AMP) that the person who dwells in the secret place of the Most High shall remain stable and fixed under the shadow of the Almighty. Help me to remember that my physical self may be in the midst of all kinds of trials and stressful situations, but my mind, soul, heart, and spirit can dwell with You, safely enveloped in Your perfect peace.*

LETTING THE PEACE OF CHRIST RULE IN YOUR HEART

Reading in *Awakened*
Pgs. 153-165

Opening Reflection
What emotions are often created by a need for control?
How do those emotions conflict with the biblical command to let
the peace of Christ rule in our hearts (Col 3:15)?

Notes

What God's Word Tells Us

The book of Luke records the story of two sisters who both loved Jesus but had opposite priorities. Martha was a person who enjoyed being in control. She felt overwhelmed with all the things she had to do when Jesus was on His way to her house. She wanted the rooms to be spotless, the food to be delicious, and for her guest to be impressed with how she managed to do it all. Her sister Mary took the opposite approach. She was so excited that food and dusty floors were the last things on her mind. Everything that needed to be done just faded away, because what could be more important than spending time with Jesus? Talk about the principle of separate realities!

When Jesus arrived, Mary just plopped herself down at His feet and tuned everything else out. "But Martha was distracted with much serving. And she went up to Him and said, 'Lord, do you not care that my sister has left me to serve alone? Tell her then to help me'" (Luke 10:40 ESV). You can imagine what she was thinking: *Why am I the only one who gets things done around here?! Everything would fall apart without me! How can I relax?* But Jesus said to her, "Martha, Martha, you are anxious and troubled about many things, but one thing is necessary. Mary has chosen the good portion, which will not be taken away from her" (Luke 10:41-42 ESV).

Martha wasn't wrong to care about organizing her house and being a gracious hostess. If she had served the Lord with a glad heart and not concerned herself with Mary's behaviors, she would have saved herself a lot of frustration. Jesus didn't correct her because she chose to work; the rebuke came after she expressed her anxious, resentful attitude over Mary's differing priorities. Martha chose to create a problem when there was none. She wasn't happy that things weren't going her way and probably stressed out the people around her frequently because they weren't doing what she thought they should be doing.

The "portion" Mary had chosen was good, but Martha's wasn't *bad*: taking action is important and clearly necessary for us to follow God's plan for our lives. "There is a time for everything, and a season for every activity under heaven" (Eccl 3:1). We can't sit around and float on a glory cloud all day when there is work to be done. But the book of Luke says Martha was "*distracted* with much serving." Her good works actually prevented her from connecting with God. If we cannot stop *doing* long enough to just *be*, we won't hear God's voice speaking to us. We cannot value control over the peace that comes from spending time with God and allowing His will to prevail over ours.

Be open to the Holy Spirit's leading and let God show you which things you need to act on and which you need to let go of. Give the people around you space to be themselves and do things their own way sometimes. Rather than expecting everything to make sense and follow your personal logic, appreciate the paradox and nuance in your life. Remind yourself that it's okay not to understand everything that happens. Above all, "let the peace of Christ rule in your hearts, since as members of one body you were called to peace. And be thankful" (Col 3:15).

Application Questions

Is there a task at work that you believe has only one right way to complete? Examine that area closely—is it possible to accept other methodologies and approaches?

What is something that you choose to see as a problem instead of accepting as it is? How can you reframe your thoughts about it?

Is there some aspect of your life that is important, but you've gotten out of balance and decided it is all-important and you can't be content without it? What irrational standards do you need to let go of?

What is something that is unfair or completely illogical that gets you upset? How can you change your thinking so that you don't create an emotional problem in addition to the practical problem?

Are there any unknowns in your life that you feel you must figure out in order to have peace? What biblical truths can help you be okay with not knowing?

Additional Scripture

Therefore I tell you, do not be anxious about your life, what you will eat or what you will drink, nor about your body, what you will put on. Is not life more than food, and the body more than clothing? Look at the birds of the air: they neither sow nor reap nor gather into barns, and yet your heavenly Father feeds them. Are you not of more value than they?

And which of you by being anxious can add a single hour to his span of life? And why are you anxious about clothing? Consider the lilies of the field, how they grow: they neither toil nor spin, yet I tell you, even Solomon in all his glory was not arrayed like one of these.

(Matt 6:25-34 ESV)

"To Do" Challenge

Make a t-chart. On the left side, write down a few things that frustrate you or make you lose your peace because you don't have control over them. On the right side, note the related aspects that you *do* have control over. For example, you can't control whether or not students are motivated to learn. You *can* control your reaction to their lack of motivation: whether you get mad at students if they don't participate or if you continue supporting them. You can also control whether you create engaging lessons and try to incorporate students' interests whenever possible. Shift your focus from the things that you can't control to the things that you can, and make a conscious decision to do so when you're talking with other educators about perceived problems.

Prayer: *Jesus, help me not to resist reality. Remind me that I'm complaining and getting annoyed over situations that You allowed or placed in my life. Ultimately, God, You are concerned with my heart attitude and my spiritual growth, not my comfort. Shift my priorities to align with Yours, Lord. I want to maintain my peace even when I feel totally helpless and out of control. I trust You, and I submit to You. Your word says, "As the heavens are higher than the earth, so are My ways higher than your ways, and My thoughts than your thoughts" (Isa 55:8-9). Take my mind off the silly earthly problems, and the big stuff that only You can comprehend. Let Your peace be the ruler of my heart. No matter what happens today, this is the day which You have made; I will rejoice and be glad in it (Ps 118:24 NKJV).*

BELIEVE THE BEST WITH A POSITIVE SENTIMENT OVERRIDE:

STIRRING UP LOVE AND COMPASSION

Reading in *Awakened*
Pgs. 166-174

Opening Reflection
What is the difference between believing the best about people and being naïve?

Notes

What God's Word Tells Us

Most of us understand on an intellectual level that believing the best is a loving perspective to have. Yet we don't practice that principle because we lose sight of the fact that love is the foundation of Christianity. Without love, we have *nothing*. Love is the gospel in a nutshell. God *is* love, and love *is* God. If we really understood this—if God's love was something we truly meditated on and sought to comprehend more than anything else—we would live our lives much differently. Love is always the answer, no matter what the question.

The negative thoughts we have about people and our circumstances may be true. But they don't release God's power into the situation. They don't ready us to be a vessel God can use and an instrument of His love. The prophet Isaiah wrote, "The Lord has given me a strong warning not to think like everyone else does. He said, 'Don't call everything a conspiracy, like they do, and don't live in dread of what frightens them. Make the Lord of Heaven's Armies holy in your life. He is the One you should fear. He is the One who should make you tremble'" (Isa 8:11-13 NLT). Out of reverential fear of God and respect for His power, we shouldn't worry about being taken advantage of by people, but speak biblical life and truth over our situations.

Our fear of getting hurt fades away when we are filled with the spirit of love. Colossians 3:12-14 tells us, "Therefore, as God's chosen people, holy and dearly loved, clothe yourselves with compassion, kindness, humility, gentleness and patience. Bear with each other and forgive one another if any of you has a grievance against someone. Forgive as the Lord forgave you. And over all these virtues put on love, which binds them all together in perfect unity." This scripture is describing deliberate acts: *clothe* yourselves and *put on* love. Your clothes don't hop onto your body in the morning, and you probably don't wake up feeling patient and kind. Just like clothing, our attitude must be selected on a daily basis and intentionally used to cover us.

Verses 16-17 continue, "Let the message of Christ dwell among you richly as you teach and admonish one another with all wisdom through psalms, hymns, and songs from the Spirit, singing to God with gratitude in your hearts. And whatever you do, whether in word or deed, do it all in the name of the Lord Jesus, giving thanks to God the Father through Him." We don't have to maintain a spirit of peace and gratitude by ourselves; we can lean on the support of a community of believers. We can keep our focus on working for the Lord by listening to and singing praise music, and talking about what God is doing in our lives. Again, these are actions we have to choose to take. Various translations of 2 Timothy 1:6 refer to *stirring up, fanning the flame,* and *kindling afresh* the faith and love we are gifted from God: "Therefore I remind you to stir up the gift of God which is in you through the laying on of hands … Surround yourself with positive people who have a Godly outlook; pray for and encourage one another."

Don't wait until you feel like being loving—stir up those feelings! Counteract those who like to "stir the pot" by stirring up love! Make it your personal mission to believe the best about every person you come across. In all things, be compelled by the love of Christ (2 Cor 5:14). Allow His love—not your feelings, not skepticism, not cynicism—to control you. Ask our heavenly Father to make His presence known to you, so that His love will be so all-encompassing, so overwhelming, and so unfathomable that you cannot help but let it impact every aspect of your teaching.

Application Questions

In what areas of your life do you struggle with cynicism?

Are there thoughts you've had recently about a person or situation that are true but not productive? What are some productive, loving thoughts you can replace those with?

Think of a time when you believed the best about someone and were taken advantage of. What does God tell us to do in those situations—how are we to respond to that person and others in the future?

How can you stay optimistic and believe the best in situations that are not likely to improve or resolve themselves?

What are some ways you can stir up love within yourself? How can your community of believers support one another in this?

Additional Scripture

If I speak in the tongues of men and of angels, but have not love, I am a noisy gong or a clanging cymbal …

Love is patient and kind; love does not envy or boast; it is not arrogant or rude. It does not insist on its own way; it is not irritable or resentful; it does not rejoice at wrongdoing, but rejoices with the truth. Love bears all things, believes all things, hopes all things, endures all things …

So now faith, hope, and love abide, these three; but the greatest of these is love.

(1 Cor 13:1, 4-7, 13 ESV)

"To Do" Challenge

Think of a student (or other person at your school) toward whom you have a negative sentiment override: this may be someone that you subconsciously "have it out for" or get upset just from seeing or thinking about him or her. To train yourself to rely on positive sentiment overrides and act in a more loving way, make a list of at least ten good qualities about that person. You might also write down facts about the person that stir up kindness and compassion in you, such as personal struggles that s/he is dealing with or obstacles that s/he must overcome. Read the list to yourself each time you think something negative about that person—speak the words out loud whenever possible. The more often you choose thoughts that create feelings of compassion, the easier it will be for you to believe the best and remove the stress and tension that are created by a negative, cynical attitude.

Prayer: *Father, thank You for Your perfect love that equips us to love each other. You tell us in Your word that love covers a multitude of sins (1 Pet 4:8); it doesn't rejoice at wrongdoing and take pleasure in sharing it. Love tries to make things better. Help me to respond to others' shortcomings with humility and compassion. Make the heights and depths of Your love real in my life: show me that Your love is great enough to heal me from any wound. I don't have to fear being hurt by people, because Your perfect love drives out fear (1 John 4:18). Even if I am perceived as naïve or am taken advantage of by others, I know that I am blessed, for it is better to suffer for doing good than for doing evil (1 Pet 3:13-17). Help me to bear with people and forgive them, just as You bear with and forgive me. Stir up Your love afresh in me. Let Your love compel and control me.*

TRAIN YOURSELF TO BE DIFFICULT TO OFFEND:

CHOOSING TO BE
SLOW TO ANGER

Reading in *Awakened*
Pgs. 175-181

Opening Reflection
How can a proper perspective on humility and our identity in Christ keep us from
being easily offended or angered?

Notes

What God's Word Tells Us

Have you noticed that when God says *don't*, He really means, *don't hurt yourself*? There's often a great personal advantage to us when we follow His plan, and dealing with offenses is a perfect example. Though taking offense is a natural reaction when people push our buttons or make little digs at us, it actually steals our joy. We think we're punishing the other person by getting mad, but it's actually ourselves that we're harming. That's why Proverbs 19:11 tells us, "A person's wisdom yields patience; it is to one's glory to overlook an offense." The ASV translates it this way: "The discretion of a man maketh him slow to anger; and it is his glory to pass over a transgression."

In John 8:3-5 (NKJV), Jesus shows us how to tap into our God-given wisdom when faced with offense: "Then the scribes and Pharisees brought to Him a woman caught in adultery ... they said to Him, 'Teacher, this woman was caught in adultery, in the very act. Now Moses, in the law, commanded us that such should be stoned. But what do You say?' This they said, testing Him, that they might have something of which to accuse Him." Can't you just picture the Pharisees' smug self-righteousness as they purposely set Jesus up to be embarrassed and proven wrong?

You might already know the now-infamous line Jesus utters in response. However, look what He does *before* He speaks: "But Jesus stooped down and wrote on the ground with His finger, as though He did not hear" (John 8:6). Jesus might have been tempted to take offense, but if so, He didn't immediately rush to set the Pharisees straight. He *readied* Himself to act with mercy and compassion. He *chose* to follow the example of God the Father, who is longsuffering, slow to wrath, compassionate, and merciful (Exod 34:6). And when Jesus finally did speak, His words indicate He was motivated by love and not by the desire to prove Himself.

In the next three verses of John 8 we read, "So when they continued asking Him, He raised Himself up and said to them, 'He who is without sin among you, let him throw a stone at her first.' And again He stooped down and wrote on the ground. Then those who heard it, being convicted by their conscience, went out one by one, beginning with the oldest even to the last. And Jesus was left alone, and the woman standing in the midst." This is the behavior of one who is grounded in Spirit and truth. Jesus didn't let other people get to Him. He didn't argue His point or try to prove that He was right. He let other people's *consciences* convict them—and we can do the same.

Don't allow your pride to cause you to think and act in ways that steal your joy. Refuse to forfeit your peace of mind because you have the "right" to defend yourself. When people offend you, pause and pray before deciding how to respond. Ask God to show others the error of their ways, and give you the discretion to act out of wisdom and love rather than anger. "My dear brothers and sisters, take note of this: Everyone should be quick to listen, slow to speak and slow to become angry, because human anger does not produce the righteousness that God desires. Therefore, get rid of all moral filth and the evil that is so prevalent and humbly accept the word planted in you, which can save you" (James 1:19-21).

Application Questions

In what types of situations are you most apt to forfeit your peace because you are so determined to defend yourself?

In which of those situations would it be better to remain silent? What thoughts can you think during those times to help you hold your peace?

Are you known as a thick-skinned person who responds to others with grace? What offenses do you need to start overlooking for the sake of letting peace rule in your heart?

When being assertive or correcting someone, how can you keep a positive, loving attitude so that you don't carry the emotional burden of fixing people or become influenced by pride?

Additional Scripture

Surely there is not a righteous man on earth who does good and never sins. Do not take to heart all the things that people say, lest you hear your servant cursing you. Your heart knows that many times you yourself have cursed others.

(Eccl 7:20-22 ESV)

But I say to you, do not resist the one who is evil. But if anyone slaps you on the right cheek, turn to him the other also. And if anyone would sue you and take your tunic, let him have your cloak as well. And if anyone forces you to go one mile, go with him two miles.

(Matt 5:39-41).

"To Do" Challenge

Think of a situation in which someone spoke offensive words that still bother you. Remind yourself that this person was trying to express something that is both important to them and correct on *some* level. Can you identify the part of what they said that's true? Write down a reframing so that you can think those thoughts instead of replaying and rehearsing the conflict. Let go of the person's words that were based on their distorted thoughts and focus on acknowledging the heart of the matter in which there is some truth. You may want to re-read some scriptures about stirring up love and being humble, tenderhearted and full of mercy. The examples on pgs. 178-180 in *Awakened* can help you, as well.

Prayer: *Lord, help me to be slow to wrath and hold my peace. I choose to be a person who is difficult to offend, because Your word says that love is not irritable or easily offended, and keeps no record of wrongs (1 Cor 13:5 NLT). Thank You for showing me that kind of love! You are a compassionate and gracious God, slow to anger, abounding in love and faithfulness (Ps 86:15). Help me to love others that way. Convict me with Your Holy Spirit to keep quiet when my fleshly nature is in control and speak up when I am motivated by love. Give me a tender and humble heart so I am ready to act with mercy. Remind me that my identity is not in what other people think, but in Christ, and that You are the only One whose opinion of me matters.*

PRACTICE FORGIVENESS WHEN YOU DON'T FEEL LIKE IT:

LOVING YOUR ENEMIES AND LETTING GOD AVENGE

Reading in *Awakened*
Pgs. 182-189

Opening Reflection
How can Christians make forgiveness a way of life?

What are the advantages of doing so?

Notes

What God's Word Tells Us

The world requires us to only be loving toward the people who are loving toward us. And yet Jesus commands us, "Love your enemies and pray for those who persecute you, so that you may be sons of your Father who is in heaven. For He makes His sun rise on the evil and on the good, and sends rain on the just and on the unjust. For if you love those who love you, what reward do you have? Do not even the tax collectors do the same? And if you greet only your brothers, what more are you doing than others? Do not even the Gentiles do the same?" (Matt 5:43-47 ESV)

That's a difficult passage to cling to when you are hurting, but there's a very comforting piece of wisdom buried in the middle: "He makes His sun rise on the evil and on the good." What does God make rise? Not *the* sun; *His* sun. Jesus is reminding us of the sovereignty of God: blessings are His alone and He distributes them as He sees best. When others wrong us, we don't have to wonder, "Why me?" We sometimes experience emotional pain because we live in a fallen world where good and bad things happen to everyone … and God's sovereign plan is not thwarted by any of it.

Romans 12:17-18 (ESV) explains how we ought to behave when we are wronged: "Repay no one evil for evil, but give thought to do what is honorable in the sight of all. If possible, so far as it depends on you, live peaceably with all." You cannot control others' reactions, but you can pursue peace with them and maintain a spirit of peace within yourself. Verses 19-21 continue with a special promise that God will defend us: "Beloved, never avenge yourselves, but leave it to the wrath of God, for it is written, 'Vengeance is mine, I will repay, says the Lord.' On the contrary, if your enemy is hungry, feed him; if he is thirsty, give him something to drink; for by so doing you will heap burning coals on his head. Do not be overcome by evil, but overcome evil with good."

You might be imagining those burning coals as punishment for the person who hurt you. But consider the scripture's context. What if you thought of the coals as the flame of God's love toward others which can melt a hardened heart? God works like a refiner's fire (Mal 3:2-3): the heat gets people's attention and stirs them out of their own complacency, bringing them toward righteousness. And isn't that the ultimate goal? If it's not—if you are experiencing prolonged, all-encompassing anger about wrongs that have not been righted—that's a sign that you have lost sight of God's proclivity for justice. When you truly believe that God will seek vengeance on your behalf, it will be much easier to behave in a loving, forgiving way, because the idea of God being against someone is a terrifying prospect: "It is a fearful thing to fall into the hands of the living God" (Heb 10:31 ESV).

The magnitude of evil in this world and the sheer amount of hardships we must endure can feel overwhelming. But we cannot let ourselves be overcome by it. We must overcome evil with good, in our minds and in our deeds. We've read the book of Revelation, and we know the end of the story: good triumphs over evil, and all wrongdoing will one day be wiped out, forever. We are laboring for the winning side. And if God is for us, who can be against us (Rom 8:31)?

Application Questions

Jesus taught us to pray, "Forgive us our debts, as we also have forgiven our debtors" (Matt 6:12). Would you truly want God to forgive you in the same way that you have forgiven others? What unforgiveness do you need to let go of?

How do your beliefs about how other people are "supposed to" treat you contribute to your areas of unforgiveness?

Are there any people whom you have wronged and not sought forgiveness from? Are there any amends God is calling you to make in order to "do what is honorable" and "as far as it depends on you, live peaceably with all"?

What would total forgiveness look like in your life? How would your thoughts and conversations about the incident(s) change? To what extent would the relationship(s) be restored?

Additional Scripture

Then Peter came up and said to Him, "Lord, how often will my brother sin against me, and I forgive him? As many as seven times?" Jesus said to him, "I do not say to you seven times, but seventy times seven."

(Matt 18:21-22 ESV)

Blessed are the merciful, for they shall receive mercy. Blessed are the pure in heart, for they shall see God. Blessed are the peacemakers, for they shall be called sons of God. Blessed are those who are persecuted for righteousness' sake, for theirs is the kingdom of heaven.

(Matt 5:7-10 ESV)

"To Do" Challenge

Unforgiveness is a burden that steals our joy and keeps us from accomplishing everything God wants to do in our lives. Anything that keeps us from serving God has got to go! Make a determination that you will no longer harbor bitterness, and ask God to reveal any unforgiveness you are not aware of (such as passive-aggressive or complaining remarks you've made repeatedly about people.) Are you still thinking and talking about a minor offense someone made against you a long time ago? Go to the Lord and humbly ask for His forgiveness, and ask Him how He would like you to live peaceably with others. Write down a reframing for the incident so that anytime you are tempted to think or say something that reveals an unforgiving heart, you can re-read your new perspective.

Prayer: *Jesus, You have commanded us to love one another as You have loved us (John 13:34 ESV). I need You to give me a merciful spirit, Lord. I choose to humble myself before You and others, and I am actively deciding to be gracious. I want to be known as Your disciple not because I go around preaching and telling other people how to live, but because of the way I love others (John 13:35). I know that the most loving way to respond to someone who has wronged me is to forgive them. I claim the power to do that in Your name. Prompt me to seek forgiveness when I offend others or act rudely and selfishly. I have been forgiven much; help me to love much (Luke 7:47). Let the example of my loving actions lead other people to You, Lord. I choose to live peaceably with all, as far as it depends on me.*

DECIDE AHEAD OF TIME HOW YOU'RE GOING TO ACT:

COMMITTING YOUR WORKS TO THE LORD

Reading in *Awakened*
Pgs. 190-195

Opening Reflection
What does it mean to act on the good that is inside of you instead of the problems that are surrounding you?

Notes

What God's Word Tells Us

Isn't it wonderful that we don't have to wait for our thoughts to be Godly to behave in a Godly way? Proverbs 16:3 (NKJV) tells us, "Commit your works to the Lord and your thoughts will be established." You can make the commitment to live according to God's plan despite how you think or feel, and eventually your thoughts and emotions will catch up. This is a pro-active determination consisting of three steps which you can follow all throughout your life: preparing your mind for action, walking in the Spirit, and using God's word to come against the enemy and your flesh.

Being pro-active means you're not waiting to see what happens and reacting to it; you're getting ready in advance. That's the first step. 1 Peter 1:13 (ESV) says, "Therefore, preparing your minds for action, and being sober-minded, set your hope fully on the grace that will be brought to you at the revelation of Jesus Christ." Peter tells us to *prepare* our minds for whatever acts we will need to carry out, with a sober, realistic mindset. And we're not instructed to place our hope in having life go smoothly or having all of our problems resolved, but rather, in the fact that Jesus will one day return and be revealed to all humankind. Now *that's* the kind of steadfast, eternal perspective that makes it so much easier to endure setbacks!

The second step in committing your works to the Lord is walking in the Spirit, not in the flesh (Gal 5:16). Remind yourself that you are fully empowered to do everything God asks you to. If you were working on your own to act like a perfectly ethical or moral person, that would be extremely difficult, because you'd have to become something that you aren't. Living as a follower of Jesus, however, is the process of becoming who you already *are*. Right now in this moment, through Christ, you are completely equipped to act with wisdom and discernment and love. You don't have to waste a single moment worrying about whether you'll be able to handle the problems of life! "For God gave us a spirit not of fear but of power and love and self-control" (2 Tim 1:7 ESV). That means you can respond to *every* situation by walking in the spirit of those characteristics that have already been given to you by God's grace.

The third ongoing, pro-active step in committing your works to the Lord is using scripture to come against the enemy and fight the desires of your flesh. During Jesus' forty day fast in the desert (Matt 4:1-11), Satan tried to convince Him to do all kinds of things that were contrary to the word of God. This attack came when Jesus was physically weak and therefore the most vulnerable to His emotions. But Jesus acted upon the word of God which was hidden in His heart, and repeated scripture back. We see no evidence that He was fearful of not being able to stand against the enemy. His response was basically this: *The stuff I'm hearing doesn't agree with the word of God, so I'm not reacting to it. Satan has no power over me.*

Jesus was our ultimate example of how to be pro-active instead of reactive when under stress: He prepared His mind for action, walked in the spirit of power and self-control, and used God's word to counter the enemy. When you are tempted to behave in ways that you (and God) will not be satisfied with later, commit your works to the Lord by speaking His word over your situation. Announce that you are going to follow the Lord no matter how you feel, and act on the Spirit-wrought character that is in you instead of reacting to circumstances. Because of Christ's sacrifice on the cross, you can proclaim the blood of Jesus over any forces that come against you, and act rather than react. No matter how you feel, the truth is that you are not fighting *for* victory, but *from* victory. You are more than a conqueror in Christ (Rom 8:37).

Application Questions

In what ways do you allow circumstances and others' actions to influence yours instead of sticking with your commitment to serve God?

What are some potentially stressful situations for which you need to mentally prepare so that you can act rather than react?

What scriptural truths can you think and speak in those situations?

Additional Scripture

I rejoice in following Your statutes as one rejoices in great riches. I meditate on Your precepts and consider Your ways. I delight in Your decrees; I will not neglect Your word …

Give me understanding, so that I may keep Your law and obey it with all my heart. You are my portion, Lord; I have promised to obey Your words. I have sought Your face with all my heart; be gracious to me according to Your promise. I have considered my ways and have turned my steps to Your statutes. I will hasten and not delay to obey Your commands …

Direct my footsteps according to Your word; let no sin rule over me.

(Ps 119:14-16, 57-60, 133)

"To Do" Challenge

Think about some productive behavioral habits that you can create to make it easier for you to prepare your mind for action, walk in the Spirit, and use God's word to come against the enemy and your flesh. What practices can you put into place to help you behave as the victorious son or daughter of the King? List a few actions you'd like to implement on a regular basis—even when you don't feel like doing them—and identify some routines you can build to make those actions more habitual. As you implement them, reflect on how the practice of committing your works to the Lord has established your thought life.

Prayer: *Lord, I ask You to prepare my heart and mind for whatever situations You have in store for me today. Give me the wisdom to follow the Spirit rather my flesh. Prompt me to think about Your word continually: may the words of my mouth and the meditation of my heart be pleasing in Your sight, oh Lord, my rock and my redeemer (Ps 19:14). I commit this day to You, and invite You to direct my steps. Tell me the ways I should go: whether I turn to the right or to the left, let my ears hear a voice behind me saying, "This is the way; walk in it" (Isa 30:21). Help me to remember that in Christ, I am a new creation, and an ambassador for You (2 Cor 5:17-21 ESV). Empower me so that I can walk worthy of that calling, Father. Thank You for Your word, Your love, Your power, and Your sacrifice for me.*

ACCEPT THAT YOU'LL NEVER GET IT <u>ALL</u> RIGHT:

WALKING AS CHILDREN OF LIGHT

Reading in *Awakened*

Pgs. 196-202

Opening Reflection

Think of a person in the Bible who was used by God in powerful ways (such as Moses, Abraham, David, or one of the disciples.) How did the Lord work through that person's weaknesses and mistakes to accomplish great things?

Notes

What God's Word Tells Us

The scripture that initially inspired the *Awakened* title was Ephesians 5:8-14 (NKJV). It reads: "For you were once darkness, but now you are light in the Lord. Walk as children of light (for the fruit of the Spirit is in all goodness, righteousness, and truth), finding out what is acceptable to the Lord. And have no fellowship with the unfruitful works of darkness, but rather expose them ... all things that are exposed are made manifest by the light, for whatever makes manifest is light. Therefore He says: 'Awake, you who sleep, arise from the dead, and Christ will give you light.'"

We who are in the light of Christ have been awakened. We are no longer dead in our sins and works of darkness: we have been illuminated and have now *become* the light ourselves! Matthew 5:13-16 tells us, "You are the light of the world. A town built on a hill cannot be hidden. Neither do people light a lamp and put it under a bowl. Instead they put it on its stand, and it gives light to everyone in the house. In the same way, let your light shine before others, that they may see your good deeds and glorify your Father in heaven."

The light of Jesus now shines in and through us, so our task is to *walk* as children of light each day. It's a daily decision and an ongoing choice to put off our old selves and put on our new selves. Ephesians 4:17-24 (ESV) tells us, " ... you must no longer walk as the Gentiles do, in the futility of their minds. They are darkened in their understanding ... But that is not the way you learned Christ ... to put off your old self, which belongs to your former manner of life and is corrupt through deceitful desires, and to be renewed in the spirit of your minds, and to put on the new self, created after the likeness of God in true righteousness and holiness."

When you put off your old self that was darkened in understanding and instead walk in the light, each setback becomes a chance to rely on God and let Him grow you. Though there is pain in the process of growing, it is far preferable to the pain of being spiritually stagnant and stuck in our bad habits. In His kindness, God doesn't try to change everything about us at once. Instead, He sheds light on just a few areas at a time, working patiently to continually help us grow. So when the Lord illuminates your shortcomings, be grateful! Follow His leading with gladness and be compassionate with yourself, just as He is loving and patient toward you. Allow joy, peace, and contentment to fill your heart, knowing that these feelings are not the end goal we hope to experience if we eventually get what we want, but rather the effects of a life spent serving God *right now*.

When you feel like you're not making progress, remind yourself of Galatians 6:9 (ESV): "And let us not grow weary of doing good, for in due season we will reap, if we do not give up." There are so many wonderful things ahead if you stay the course. God has foreseen your trials and will use them to strengthen you and bring you closer to Him. He has planned your breakthroughs and each instance of deliverance in His perfect timing. Keep walking in the light, as He is in the light (1 John 1:7). Look to the Lord to guide your every step and continually bring you closer to Him: "Let us acknowledge the Lord; let us press on to acknowledge Him. As surely as the sun rises, He will appear; He will come to us like the winter rains, like the spring rains that water the earth" (Hos 6:3).

Application Questions

Do you have a "thorn in the flesh" weakness like Paul (2 Cor 12:7-10) that you believe God has placed in your life? Is there anything you are resisting that God has assigned you to deal with?

In what areas of your life are your expectations far too high for yourself?

Why is it important to remind yourself that each setback is a chance to practice what you have learned and depend more fully on God? What benefits will you experience?

What can you do to encourage yourself in the daily process of renewing your mind?

Additional Scripture

… There was given me a thorn in the flesh, a messenger of Satan to torment me—to keep me from exalting myself! Concerning this I implored the Lord three times that it might leave me. And He has said to me, "My grace is sufficient for you, for power is perfected in weakness."

Most gladly, therefore, I will rather boast about my weaknesses, so that the power of Christ may dwell in me. Therefore I am well content with weaknesses, with insults, with distresses, with persecutions, with difficulties, for Christ's sake; for when I am weak, then I am strong.

(2 Cor 12:7-10 NASB)

"To Do" Challenge

Reflect on any thoughts and habits that create unhappiness in your life. What negativity do you need to let go of in order to make room for happiness? What needs to be removed from your life so you can be everything God created you to be? Choose one area you feel like God is calling you to grow in, and take on the adventure of following His leading. After you finish this book, embark on a mission to read more scriptures on your selected topic. Do a search online for Biblical resources that can support you in shifting your perspective and developing a Christ-like mindset. Train yourself to look forward to this time of reflection: expect God to show up and do a mighty work in your life!

Prayer: *Lord, I thank You for making me aware of the areas in which I fall short of Your standard. Thank You for loving me enough to correct me and bring me up to a higher level. Thank You for giving me trials so that I can become more like You. It's not easy for me to work through my issues, but because of Your great love, I will not be consumed; Your mercies are new every morning, and great is Your faithfulness (Lam 3:22-23). I ask You to continue renewing my mind day by day. Help me to look to You as I walk in Your light. Let others see the light you've placed in me, and may it bring glory to Your name.*

AFTERWORD

THE SELF-TALK OF AN AWAKENED TEACHER:

RELYING ON GOD AS THE UNCHANGING ROCK

Reading in *Awakened*

Pgs. 203-208

Opening Reflection

What are some characteristics of God that we can depend on,
no matter what is happening in our lives?

Notes

What God's Word Tells Us

It often seems like the only thing we can count on for sure in education is that something unexpected will happen. Just when we've mastered one curriculum, another is introduced. Right when we've got our routines running somewhat smoothly, a new student is added. Or our schedule is changed. Or a new assessment method is introduced. We get our minds geared up to face the day, and then a new problem hits us from out of nowhere and we get thrown completely off track.

What a blessing and comfort it is to know that there is one aspect of our life that will never change: "Jesus Christ is the same yesterday, today, and forever" (Heb 13:8). We also read in Malachi 3:6 (KJV): "For I am the Lord, I change not; therefore ye sons of Jacob are not consumed." Unlike human beings, God does not retract His promises or fail to come through. He doesn't give us one instruction today and tell us to do things differently tomorrow. Whatever He has said is true for all time, and what He says He will do, He'll do! "Every good gift and every perfect gift is from above, and comes down from the Father of lights, with whom there is no variation or shadow of turning" (James 1:17 NKJV).

Though we would love to be as stable and unchanging as the Lord, our weaknesses and emotional shortcomings can be used to show people the greatness of our God. In 2 Corinthians 4:7-9, we are compared to earthen jars: fragile, breakable, unremarkable, and yet containing something of immense value: "But we have this treasure in jars of clay to show that this all-surpassing power is from God and not from us. We are hard pressed on every side, but not crushed; perplexed, but not in despair; persecuted, but not abandoned; struck down, but not destroyed." Our resilience does not come from or depend on our physical selves, but from what God has placed inside us, which can never be taken away or destroyed. The cracks in our humble earthen jars let God's light shine through more brightly.

The chapter in 2 Corinthians continues, "Therefore we do not lose heart. Though outwardly we are wasting away, yet inwardly we are being renewed day by day. For our light and momentary troubles are achieving for us an eternal glory that far outweighs them all. So we fix our eyes not on what is seen, but on what is unseen. For what is seen is temporary, but what is unseen is eternal" (2 Cor 4:16-18). Our physical bodies and the things around us on earth are only momentary and fading away, but on the inside, we are being continually renewed. The work God is doing in us will last forever. Every trial we face in this lifetime will be far outweighed by the lavish celebration that's coming in heaven.

When the annoyances and disturbances in life get you down, trust in the Lord, your everlasting rock (Isa 26:4 ESV). Take your focus off today's problems, which will soon be a distant memory, and fix your eyes on the eternal. There is *nothing* that can keep you from the loving plan your Heavenly Father has for you in eternity: "For I am sure that neither death nor life, nor angels nor rulers, nor things present nor things to come, nor powers, nor height nor depth, nor anything else in all creation, will be able to separate us from the love of God in Christ Jesus our Lord" (Rom 8:38-39 ESV).

Application Questions

How has God made Himself known to you and renewed your mind during the course of this study? You may want to spend some time looking back over the previous application questions and reflecting on your growth and the way God has answered your prayers. Use the blank note-taking pages that follow if needed. Specifically, think about how your mindset has changed in the following areas as you've grown closer to God:

- My awareness of and response to my thoughts
- My self image
- My explanatory style
- My strategies for dealing with conflict
- My behavioral habits
- My relationship with the past
- My standards and expectations
- My mental habits
- My emotional stability
- My behavioral habits and lifestyle
- My prayer life
- My love walk

In which of these areas (or other areas) have you seen the greatest personal transformation? In what areas would you most like to focus on growing next?

Additional Scripture

I will love You, O Lord my strength. The Lord is my rock and my fortress and my deliverer; my God, my strength, in whom I will trust; my shield and the horn of my salvation, my stronghold. I will call upon the Lord, who is worthy to be praised; so shall I be saved from my enemies …

For You will light my lamp; the Lord my God will enlighten my darkness. For by You I can run against a troop, by my God I can leap over a wall. As for God, His way is perfect; the word of the Lord is proven; He is a shield to all who trust in Him. For who is God, except the Lord? And who is a rock, except our God? It is God who arms me with strength, and makes my way perfect.

(Ps 18:1-3, 18-32 NKJV)

"To Do" Challenge

If you have ever kept a prayer journal, you know what a powerful tool it can be in helping you see the results of entrusting your life to God. Write down your prayer requests today, and set up a regular schedule for doing so again. You might want to prayer journal once a week or once a month, setting a specific day so it becomes a habit. Each time you revisit your previous requests, write down how God has worked in that situation. In the scenarios in which you have not yet seen a direct answer to prayer, reflect on the renewal of your mind and your spiritual growth. How has God used that prayer request and heart's desire to draw you closer to Him and transform you more into His image? When you become discouraged, revisit your prayer journal and stir up gratitude as you see the ways God has come through for you. You may even want to record some examples of answered prayer that occurred before you started prayer journaling, and re-read those stories to encourage and inspire you to keep pressing on in God.

Prayer: *Dear Father, thank You for drawing me to this study and speaking to me through it. Thank You for renewing and transforming me day by day. Thank You for being my solid rock in a world of sinking sand. Help me to keep my eyes fixed on You. I know that You will keep me in perfect peace when my mind is stayed on You and I trust in You (Isa 26:3 ESV). Continue to work in me, Lord. Show me what to do next so that I keep growing in You. Lead, teach, and guide me, Father. I want to be everything You say I can be in Christ. Use me in my work and in my personal life so I can be an instrument of Your love. Here am I, Lord, send me (Isa 6:8)!*

NOTES

NOTES

NOTES

NOTES

NOTES

NOTES

PRINTABLE SCRIPTURE AND PRAYER POSTERS

Memorizing God's word is a critical part of renewing your mind. To help with this, I've compiled the scripture references and prayers into a PDF document. There's one page for each devotion. You can reference the pages on your phone, tablet, or computer. Or, print them out as a set of mini posters: keep them tucked in your lesson plan book, hang them on your refrigerator at home and read them each morning, or display them somewhere else where they can encourage and remind you of God's truth.

This is a really powerful tool for allowing scripture to permeate your thinking. If you're completing the devotional on a weekly schedule, you can keep the corresponding scripture page displayed and read it over each day. After you've completed the study, you can continue to cycle through the pages, reading and reflecting on a different one each day or week so that the words are made fresh once again in your mind and heart.

Visit TheCornerstoneForTeachers.com/books/awakened-devotional to download the posters for free.

ONLINE BIBLE STUDY INFORMATION

Are you looking for a group of Christian educators to work through this devotional with you? Join the online Bible study and book club for *The Awakened Devotional Study Guide for Christian Educators*! One devotion is posted on a private blog each week, and participants respond to the questions in the comments. You can share as much or as little as you'd like. Let the group know what your prayer requests are and learn from one another's journeys and struggles. Visit TheCornerstoneForTeachers.com/books/awakened-devotional to find out more details and see when the next online Bible study for teachers is starting.

ABOUT THE AUTHOR

ANGELA WATSON (formerly Powell) is passionate about sharing practical, relevant teacher resources. She was a National Board Certified classroom teacher for eleven years, creating her first website in 2003 to provide behavior management strategies, teaching techniques, and organizational tips. In 2008, the site was expanded and renamed TheCornerstoneForTeachers.com in coordination with the publication of her first book, *The Cornerstone: Classroom Management That Makes Teaching More Effective, Efficient, and Enjoyable.*

Now as founder and owner of Due Season Press and Educational Services, Angela conducts a wide range of consulting services, including ongoing instructional coaching for PreK-12 teachers in New York City. She recently wrote *Awakened: Change Your Mindset to Transform Your Teaching* to help teachers develop a positive, flexible, and resilient way of thinking about the challenges of working in education. *The Awakened Devotional Study Guide for Christian Educators* is her third book.

Angela has an active web presence to support teachers worldwide in their practice. She regularly adds to the collection of free classroom resources on her website, including photos, activities, printables, and more. She maintains a blog on the site to create discussions around educational topics, and a separate blog with teacher devotions.

For more information about Angela (including professional development bookings), please visit: TheCornerstoneForTeachers.com/about.

CPSIA information can be obtained
at www.ICGtesting.com
Printed in the USA
BVHW01s1547180818
524359BV00006B/101/P